THROW AWAY YOUR RÉSUMÉ!

SECOND EDITION

Also by Robert M. Hochheiser

Don't State It...Communicate It!
How To Work For A Jerk

THROW AWAY YOUR RÉSUMÉ!

SECOND EDITION

by Robert M. Hochheiser

Barron's Educational Series, Inc.

New York • London • Toronto • Sydney

All inquiries should be addressed to:

Barron's Educational Series, Inc.
250 Wireless Boulevard
Hauppauge, New York 11788

International Standard Book No. 0-8120-4356-1
Library of Congress Catalog Card No. 89-17880

Library of Congress Cataloging-in-Publication Data
Hochheiser, Robert M., 1938-
    Throw away your résumé! / by Robert M. Hochheiser. — 2nd ed.
     p. cm.
    Includes bibliographical references.
    ISBN 0-8120-4356-1
    1. Job hunting. I. Title
HF5382.7.H6   1990
650.14 – dc20   89-17880

PRINTED IN THE UNITED STATES OF AMERICA

0123   800   9 8 7 6 5 4 3 2 1

CONTENTS

Preface

Typically, books on how to get a job are written by management recruiters, employment-agency owners, personnel managers, and career counselors. Unfortunately for job-seekers, these people are experts at hiring—not at being hired. They've never had to follow their own advice, and their background consists of meeting the needs of employers rather than achieving the goals of job applicants. Their advice to a job-seeker is therefore about as useful as would be the memoirs of a hangman to a condemned prisoner.

I found that out several years ago when a corporate reorganization transformed me from company vice-president to standee on the unemployment line. By writing what the latest books suggested would be a great résumé and being armed with a flawless track record and impeccable references, I thought I'd have another job in no time.

A thousand résumés and many months later, I was still out of work. My "luck" didn't change until I realized that the "experts" were obviously wrong. I stopped using résumés and started merchandising my services in a different way—one that works. I got several offers in short order.

Not only did I become re-employed, but I also realized that what worked for me would work for anyone. Since then, I have advised job-seekers both individually and through courses I have given at a number of colleges. In this regard, I am happy to say that engineers, teachers, salespeople, stock analysts, mechanics, executives, and secretaries have all been helped by my approach to getting hired. In the hope that even more people can avoid going through what I went through to get a job, that approach is described in detail in this book.

The biggest change in this edition is a new Chapter 12 that shows how to fine tune job applications if employers might perceive your experience as too little, too much, or not recent enough to suit them. A new "fill-in-the-blanks" approach I have developed helps you to tailor what you say to the needs of each prospective employer. In addition, new sample letters have been added to Chapter 10, and a few sentences have been revised to enhance clarity.

You'll find no untried theories here — just proven techniques that work. Use them wisely and prodigiously, and hopefully you will soon have a better job than you've ever had.

My sincerest thanks to the many thousands of people who bought the first edition of this book. Their favorable response has been most gratifying.

A torrent of thanks to my wife, Eileen. Totally supportive when I was out of work, she also typed and proofread several early drafts of this book. She has been a constant source of strength and inspiration.

Robert M. Hochheiser
Monsey, NY

A. THE CONCEPTS

1. Résumés Don't Work

Suppose someone offered to sell you a package with the following description on the label:

> Water, Laurel Sulfate, Lauramide Dea, Propylparaben, Methylparaben, Imidazolidinyl, Urea, . . .

Would that information prompt you to buy the package? Probably not. Why should you even take the time to think about it? The seller doesn't tell you what it is, what it does, or how it would benefit you.

The package described above contains *shampoo*. A manufacturer who tried to sell the package by listing only the ingredients on the label, however, would probably lose a great deal of business to another brand described as "Conditioning Shampoo—just right for *your* hair." Generally, people never look at a product's ingredients until they first see the name of the product and what it claims to offer. Then, if they are interested, they will look further.

Getting customers to look further is an integral part of effective merchandising. The advertising industry learned long ago that technical details and lists of ingredients do not provide the customer with enough motivation to ring up quick sales. That motivation is provided only by selling a product on the basis of the benefits it offers to its users.

Getting a job is similar to selling a product. *You* are the product, *prospective employers* are your customers, and a *résumé* is the list of ingredients summarizing your career. Like the shampoo manufacturer, you will find—if you haven't done so already—that résumés are the worst way to sell your services.

The following pages will show you a better way—one that works!

Your Pitch Must Make a Hit

The more often you interview, the quicker you'll meet an employer who has just what you are looking for, and the sooner you'll get that job you want. Apply to a large enough population of employers and, even with an atrociously inefficient sales pitch, you will make a connection, eventually. Imagine how much quicker you'll connect with a *good* pitch.

Why not use great numbers to your advantage so you can have a choice of good jobs from which to select? You *can* get multiple offers, but your sales pitch cannot be just good; it's got to be great. Your message to an employer must be compelling—overpoweringly compelling to the point that he or she cannot resist calling you in for an interview at the earliest opportunity.

A good job will draw as many as several hundred candidates. In such a situation, the employer will first screen all applications, discarding those who seem to be unqualified. The remaining applications are read and re-read in successive screenings until only the most promising candidates remain under consideration.

At this stage, all the employer has is a handful of paper with no knowledge of any of the candidates except the information in their applications. The most promising candidates are therefore merely those who *appear* on paper to be the best of the bunch. This is one of the keys to throwing away your résumé.

The most interviews go to those who write the best applications, and the most offers go to those who handle themselves best during interviews. Are these people the most qualified for the job? Not necessarily, but they are the best at convincing the employer that *they* would be most qualified, and that's all that is important.

Whenever you go after a job, do it as if it is a matter of dire emergency. Hold nothing back and go all out, using every facet of your knowledge and experience to impress the employer. Act as if your competition is the very best in your field. This means that you must blow your horn as loudly and as clearly as possible.

Not only do you have to compete against others, you also compete against time. An employer simply doesn't have the time to read and interpret every sentence and paragraph in a stack of applications. It's a quick glance that will make or break your chances.

If an employer has to sift through and interpret your résumé, it may not be clear to him how your "list of ingredients" would qualify you as the best candidate. The same applies if your application is too vague. When others are willing to provide details, why should the employer take the time to find out what you're all about? With any application, you'll probably get only one chance to grab the brass ring. Make that chance count, and be sure that *you* look like the best candidate.

Think Like an Employer

The first thing you have to do is to get it into your head that what you think you have to offer is of no importance whatsoever. What you think an employer should need in the way of job candidate qualifications is equally unimportant. It's what the employer thinks that counts. If you have a good gauge of what is in the mind of an employer, you can capitalize on presenting your qualifications in such a way that hiring you becomes an irresistible urge.

When it comes to getting hired, how good you are is of negligible importance compared to how good the prospective employer *thinks* you are. Even when competing for a job with people with more experience or with greater expertise than you have, if you can sell yourself better than they can, you'll stand a better chance of getting the job.

You won't be able to get any job just because you want it. Nothing in this book is fail-safe or foolproof, but if your goals are realistic, you can concentrate on reading the following pages and learn how to sell yourself to employers far more effectively than most job-seekers.

Even though you may be less than totally competent in a given area, you're a lot better off than most employers are. Although twentieth-century technology is all around us, hiring practices and techniques have not advanced in hundreds of years. Despite the application forms, references, interviews, and tests given to job candidates, hiring decisions all too often boil down to a "gut feel" as to which candidate is offered the job at what salary.

Throw Away Your Résumé will provide you with a systematic approach to getting hired. If you pursue the jobs you know you can handle and apply only on the basis of your strengths, there is no reason for you to apologize for your weaknesses. Or would you prefer to dwell on your weaknesses until you are convinced that you can't compete in the job market? The choice is yours.

Take Positive Action

Positive thinking isn't worth two cents unless it's accompanied by positive action. Here's what you have to do to get any job:

- Determine, as best you can, who would be most likely to want to make use of your talents.
- Find out, as accurately as possible, precisely what the prospective employer wants in terms of the "ideal" job candidate.
- Present a believable, documentable, and powerful case for your meeting, but not exceeding the requirements of the "ideal" candidate.
- Say whatever you have to say in order to get the job, as long as you can back it up.
- Always control communications with employers, both in written applications and in interviews, so that information obtained by the employer is to your advantage.
- Never do or say anything that might be perceived by an employer as a reason for not hiring you.
- Always have a "game plan," whether you are writing job application letters or going to an interview.

Persistence is the password for successful job-getters. Job-getters want a good job, not a good résumé, and they know that what they should be doing is job-getting—certainly not the commonly used "job-hunting." Job hunting—what's that? A sport like fox hunting?

Getting a job is definitely not a sport. At stake are your peace of mind, your need to be achieving something in life, your ability to support your family, and the basic human need to be reasonably well paid for doing work from which you derive satisfaction and enjoyment. Unless you are prepared to go about job-getting as if your life depended on it, you should expect less than outstanding results, no matter what methods you use. Regardless of whether you are currently employed, it is incumbent upon you to behave as if your timetable is immediate and your need for a job crucial. Not just any job, but a good job.

This means plenty of hard work, every day of every week, until you make the right connections. It is difficult for people to put in this level of effort if they are currently working, but unless they do, rapid success will be a matter of sheer luck.

So roll up your sleeves, and dedicate yourself to spending, if necessary, every waking hour of your available time to working at getting that job you want. If you are not willing to make a big commitment to this effort, you will have no one but yourself to blame should results be small and slow in coming.

Why and How This Method Works

The next six chapters are devoted to showing you how to conduct and organize your job search; how to motivate people to think what you want them to think; how to make a good first impression; and how to understand, recognize, and measure up to employer hiring criteria.

Those chapters, which you can think of as describing the concepts of successful job-getting, are collectively grouped together as Part A of this book. Part B, containing Chapters 8 through 14, describes specific techniques for putting those concepts to good use. Included in Part B are topics such as how and where to look for work, how to apply for jobs, how to sell your services in writing and over the telephone, what to use instead of a résumé, how to tailor your application letter to best fit the job, how to control interviews, how to size up a job, and how to negotiate with employers.

2. One Step At a Time: The System

There is only one way to climb a flight of stairs: one step at a time. Otherwise, your feet might trip over one another, you might slip, and you could hurt yourself. The path to getting a job is no different; it has to be traveled in a series of steps that must be climbed in sequence, as noted in Figure 1.

Figure 1

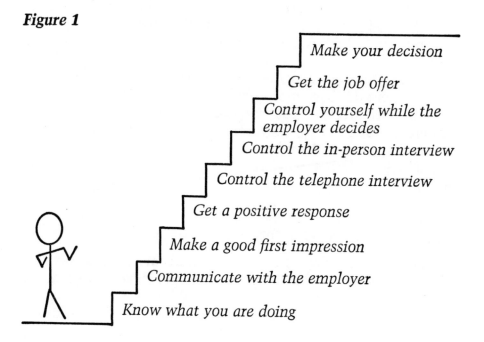

Make your decision

Get the job offer

Control yourself while the employer decides

Control the in-person interview

Control the telephone interview

Get a positive response

Make a good first impression

Communicate with the employer

Know what you are doing

KNOW WHAT YOU ARE DOING

It's one thing to know how to *do* a job and quite another to know how to *get* that job. You may be an expert at what you do for a living, but that doesn't mean that you know anything about promoting yourself and selling your services to employers.

The second part of this book is crammed with procedures for handling specific aspects of the job-getting process, but you're not ready for those yet—not if you really want to understand the reasoning behind those procedures.

Understanding the job-getting process starts with the realization that no one will hire you without meeting you; you will not get a job "sight unseen" solely on the strength of a letter or telephone call.

Getting an interview isn't that easy. Sure, there are instances in which you can walk in off the street and get an employer's ear, but those are the exceptions to the rule. Generally, employers will not even talk to you unless both of two conditions are met:

- They have a job opening.
- They have some reason to believe that meeting you would be a worthwhile use of their time.

Even if they had many openings, managers and business owners would never get anything done if they met with every job applicant who knocked at their door. Busy doing their own jobs, employers have no practical choice but to see only those candidates who seem qualified.

You will not get hired unless you first get a personal interview, and you can't do that unless you first convince an employer that you are worth meeting. You won't be able to convince anyone that you are worth meeting, however, unless you first make a good impression, and you'll not be able to do that unless you know what you're doing. *That's* why you have to travel these steps in sequence.

COMMUNICATE WITH THE EMPLOYER

Prospective employers must find out about you in a way that tells them you are available, convinces them that you are good, and compels them to want to meet with you. Who is going to do this for you . . . the butcher? the baker? maybe the candlestick maker?

You have to get the word out about yourself. This means a lot of work in terms of a great number of letters and telephone calls.

Just keep your objectives clearly in mind. You are not aiming for a job offer at this stage. The only reason you are contacting employers is to promote yourself as being someone who should be interviewed as quickly as possible. If you expect any more than that, you are in for a guaranteed disappointment.

MAKE A GOOD FIRST IMPRESSION

To make certain that meeting you is an attractive proposition, you must see to it that you are perceived as having only positive attributes, with no drawbacks. You must therefore take care to be sure that nothing negative *from the employer's point of view* is implied by what you say or what you write.

Before you start to communicate with employers, you have to realize that, having never met them, you don't know their points of view and you probably do not know a great deal about their hiring criteria. How can you say very much about yourself when you know so little about what an employer wants?

You can't. Not knowing an employer's dislikes, you might, by saying too much, inadvertently make a statement that could be viewed negatively. You should therefore restrict yourself to subjects that are pertinent and to statements that are consistent with the most basic of employer wants.

Actually, you don't have to say much at this point. All you have to do is to design your initial communication to serve merely as bait to whet the employer's appetite.

GET A POSITIVE RESPONSE

Reaching this step means that someone has taken your bait. A positive response may come in the form of a letter or telephone call asking for more information or asking you to call to schedule an interview.

When requested to arrange an interview, do so without delay. A letter asking for more information, however, gives you a perfect excuse to call the employer so *you* can ask questions to gauge his needs before you tell him anything.

By the way, if you do not reach this step with an employer, you have failed to make a good impression. Forget that employer.

Chances are you will not get a second opportunity if someone's first impression of you is negative.

CONTROL THE TELEPHONE INTERVIEW

Here's where employers start to get sneaky. They may call you claiming only to be interested in finding out when you could meet for an interview. After a few minutes of pleasant chatter, however, you find that you are being asked questions about the type of work you have done, why you are looking for a new job, and so on. Like it or not, you are being interviewed over the telephone.

You *should* like it. The telephone can put you in an excellent position to arrange an in-person interview by enabling you to learn more about what the employer wants and to further stimulate interest in seeing you.

You may be able to leap-frog directly to this step simply by using the telephone rather than the mail to apply for a job, but will people interrupt their busy schedules just to talk with you? Maybe they won't. Perhaps you will not be able to get the attention of whoever has to make hiring decisions.

You *could* get to someone by inventing some ruse, but once people suspect that they have been tricked into talking to you, your chances of getting a job from them will be reduced to someplace between zero and nonexistence.

No matter how you reach this step and no matter how good you are at controlling interviews, your objective on the telephone should *not* be to get an offer; you would be fighting a lost cause. Your real objective at this point? A face-to-face meeting.

Once you become adept at the interviewing and motivating techniques described in the following chapters, you will have a decided advantage over most employers: you will know how to control interviews in your favor, a skill they probably do not have.

CONTROL THE IN-PERSON INTERVIEW

By the time you reach this step, you should be able to learn quite a bit about the employer's needs, wants, and point of view.

Now you can go all out and push for a sale, again controlling the interview to find out as much as possible about what you have to do and say to get the job. Then all you have to do is to act accordingly.

The more interviews you get, the quicker you will be able to perfect your ability to control interviews, and the quicker you will be able to get that job you want.

CONTROL YOURSELF WHILE THE EMPLOYER DECIDES

Now that you have had what seemed like a good interview, what can you expect next?

You can expect to wait. The employer may want to meet with other candidates before making a final choice or the person you met may want you to return to meet others in the organization so they may make up their collective minds. These or any of a million other reasons can cause a hiring decision to be delayed for weeks or even months.

Don't let these delays push you out of shape. If another offer comes along while you're still waiting to hear from a particular employer, call that employer and put your cards on the table. In the event that you are really prepared to take the other offer, you have nothing to lose.

If, on the other hand, you are bluffing, you must realize that a bluff will work only when the employer has freedom to act and you are the front-running candidate. Should the person with whom you are dealing report to someone else who is the real roadblock, or should you be only one of several good candidates, the employer has no incentive to act just to suit your schedule.

Beware of bluffing. You won't look too good announcing your continued availability two months after saying that you were about to accept another offer.

GET THE OFFER

If you have done a better selling job than any other applicant, you'll get the offer. Should someone else do a better selling job, you will not get the offer. It's that simple!

MAKE YOUR DECISION

Employers who turn you down will probably not give you the real reasons for why someone else was selected, but you should always sit back and review what happened. You may be able to learn from the experience in order to do better the next time. Perhaps in retrospect you will realize that you should have done something you didn't do or that you neglected to do something you should have done.

When you *are* offered the job, you are in the driver's seat and you have three choices:

- accept the job
- negotiate for better terms
- refuse the offer

Whether you accept or refuse an offer depends upon how much you need the job, what future potential it offers, and the status of other prospects you may have at the time. Whether you negotiate for better terms depends upon whether you are prepared to settle for the original offer should the negotiation fail and also on how much you think the employer wants you.

How many stairways can you attempt to climb simultaneously? One.

How many employers can you pursue simultaneously? Hundreds.

The more employment "stairways" you identify and intelligently pursue, the faster your search will be completed.

What are you waiting for?

3. Organizing Your Job-Searching Trip

You can efficiently climb a number of employment stairways at the same time only if you are organized.

Suppose you wanted to get to the top of a large building from the ground floor. Before you rush up the nearest flight of stairs, you probably should consider using an elevator: it's faster. You would be wise, however, to make sure that elevator goes all the way to the top; maybe you need a different elevator.

The same applies to any journey you might take from one location to another. It is necessary to check whatever signs are available to make certain that you do not get detoured.

Getting a job can also be viewed as a journey: one that involves climbing a number of different stairways until one leads to a good job offer. In this regard, every journey has five major elements:

- a starting point
- a final destination
- a route of travel
- a method of traversing that route
- the resources necessary to complete the trip

On pleasure or business trips, you usually start out with a reasonably good fix on every one of these elements. This is not the case with a job-search journey.

What do you know at the start of a job search?

1. Your work experience and capabilities.
2. Your education.
3. Your current employment situation.
4. The salary you need.
5. The working conditions you would prefer.
6. Where (geographically) you would prefer to work.
7. The field of work in which you seek employment.
8. How important it is to you to find a new job.

Taken together, this information describes the starting point of your job-search journey and the resources available to you: your capabilities and the experience you offer in terms of training and career background.

The biggest problem at the start of your search is that you cannot identify your final destination with precision. You can define the type of job you want, but that isn't good enough. What you don't know are the names and addresses of those specific employers who would definitely offer you an acceptable job *if* they had an opening and *if* they were sufficiently impressed with you.

Even worse, you may not have well-defined career goals, in which case you wouldn't even be able to describe what kind of job you'd like, much less the identities of employers who might offer you work.

Not knowing their final destination, many people tend to have a tough time establishing the best route to take to find a job. Without knowing what route to take, they in turn have no way of knowing the best way of traversing that route. As a result, their efforts are about as efficient as those of a dog chasing its tail.

THINK AHEAD

Presume that you want to take a vacation. You have a certain amount of time and various likes and dislikes. How do you decide where to go? Do you call a travel agent and pick a trip at random?

Do you drive down the nearest highway until you happen to find a place you like? Or do you throw darts at a map and select your destination accordingly?

Either approach would be ridiculous. More likely, you would first research your options. Starting with a list of possibilities which appear attractive, you would select a destination, route, and mode of travel consistent with your interests as well as your time and dollar resources.

Planning a job search is no different from organizing a vacation: you have to think ahead, evaluate those alternatives most likely to result in maximum satisfaction, and take proven shortcuts whenever possible.

With a plan, you can anticipate problems and have solutions worked out and ready when you need them. Without a plan, you live by your ability to think quickly and the degree to which your gut reactions will be reliable sources of instant logic rather than emotional displays that might cloud your thinking.

To have any value at all, a plan must be in writing so that you can use it as a ready reference when necessary. Putting a plan on paper means that you won't have to worry about forgetting the fine points of your strategy.

Starting with resources, your plan should incorporate a strategy laid out around the essential elements of the job-search journey. Your resources are your strengths: the skills, capabilities, and work experiences that would be attractive to employers and thereby help you to sell your services. The following chapters will show you how to identify your work-related strengths and how to present those strengths so as to put yourself in the most attractive light.

It is necessary to start with resources because only after you establish what you have to sell can you intelligently decide who is most likely to buy. Then you can also determine what sales pitch would be most effective with each potential customer, how to get that pitch across, and what to do if it isn't working.

Another type of resource you may have are friends, relatives, or associates who may be able to introduce you to employers, provide you with references. or even offer you employment themselves.

List *all* of your resources. If you are in doubt whether a particular item or name should be listed, list it anyway.

Destinations

The destinations you should be considering are the names and addresses of those employers who would be most likely to have a need for what you offer *if* they had an opening. These are the employment stairways you should be trying to climb.

Who are these employers? Those most likely to be impressed with the resources on your list. As you will see in Chapter 9, there are several sources for the names you can put on this list. Some, in fact, may not even be names, but rather only box numbers in "blind" help-wanted advertisements.

The process of listing likely employers is never-ending. You should start with a list of no less than a hundred names, add to that list as you study current help-wanted ads, and pursue every single name on that list. If you still don't have a job when you've gone through that first list, make another and keep on going.

The key in listing destinations is the word *likely*. Why dilute your efforts when you can concentrate entirely on employers with whom you have a reasonable chance of success?

Routes

The route you choose to use is your sales pitch. For each employer you have listed, indicate on your plan which of your strengths will most likely impress that particular employer and how you could illustrate, describe, or demonstrate those strengths in a manner that will create a good impression. To do the most good, your sales pitch must be tailored to meet the needs of each employer with whom you are communicating.

You will probably find that you will come up with a number of basic sales-pitch strategies, each of which can be used with several variations. The number of strategies and strategy variations you should be using depends, of course, on the variety of jobs for which you believe you can qualify and the types of needs paramount in the minds of the different people on your list.

After establishing the strategies you plan to use, you must determine how to best implement those strategies. For any given destination, you have to decide at which step to get on the employment stairway: to write, call, or apply in person. This means designing written job applications, preparing interview game plans, and customizing every sales pitch so that it can be delivered as effectively as possible.

Consider your present situation. Almost all employers want to know what you're doing now, why you want another job, and what your current salary level is. These questions seem innocent enough at first glance, but they may trip you up unless you have the right answers prepared in advance. Employers often have rather rigid definitions of acceptability relative to an applicant's reasons for seeking new employment, to a person's current salary level, and to justifications for current or past periods of unemployment. Unless you have a good story, you may talk yourself out of a job offer before you even know it.

ACTION ITEMS AND SCHEDULES

A plan is not merely a collection of information and intentions; it's a call to action—*your* action. What are you going to do on your job search and when are you going to do it?

You have to determine what actions you can initiate and put a specific starting and completion time to each:

1. How many employers do you plan to contact every week? Which ones during which week?
2. Which employment agencies or search firms will you call or write to each week?
3. When will you make a list of friends or other people who can help? When will you contact those people?
4. What newspapers and trade journals will you read to check out help-wanted advertisements? How often will you review each source of job listings? Daily? Weekly? Monthly?
5. What follow-up method and schedule will you use with employers you contacted on an unsolicited basis? With advertisements to which you have responded? With employment agencies or other contacts?

Contingencies

You may have above-average intelligence, but you are not perfect and not likely to draw up a perfect plan. Virtually any aspect of your plan can go wrong and you must be prepared for contingencies. Contingency planning should delve into any possible result of your job search that fits both of two conditions:

- Situation has better than 50–50 chance of occurring.
- Situation could cause problem not addressed by your basic plan.

If you waited until a problem occurred before developing a way to handle that problem, you would lose valuable time (and perhaps also opportunities) because the world won't stand still while you are thinking. By planning in advance for contingencies you are recognizing the fact that certain problems occur and are putting yourself in the position of being able to smoothly shift from your basic plan to a backup plan.

A contingency plan can be related to just about any aspect of your job search. Examples are:

1. Answers to different questions you might be asked at interviews.
2. Strategy for filling out employers' application forms.
3. Alternate strategy you will use when your basic sales pitch is not producing results.
4. Alternate interview techniques for use with employers having different personality types.

Like the rest of your plan, write down the contingencies you are considering and the way you plan to deal with each situation if and when it occurs.

Updating

Don't be confused or upset if you find your plan to be in a constant state of flux. Certain items you rated as contingencies will be found to be definite probabilities and vice versa, strategies will be discarded or strengthened, and your techniques will become increasingly more effective. As you learn from experience and from your own mistakes, you will find it necessary to change your plan for the better.

Like a knife, a plan is a tool: it can cut through all the obstacles in your way to a job, but only if you keep it sharp. How do you sharpen a plan? By using it and continuing to change it until it works.

4. How Employers Think and Make Decisions

No one is hired in a vacuum. All hiring searches are conducted within the context of an employer's circumstances, starting with a determination of job objectives and functional hiring criteria.

Just as your résumé can be used to describe your current situation as a job-seeker, the circumstances of a hiring decision describe an employer's situation. These circumstances consist of five parameters, each of which can be illustrated by a series of questions:

Objectives

What functions must be performed by the person to be hired? How important are those functions? What criteria do we use to judge whether an applicant is qualified?

Risks

How sensitive is the job? What problems could be created by putting the wrong person in the job? Could I put my own job in jeopardy by hiring someone who screws up?

Alternatives

How does each applicant compare with the other applicants? Which one is best? Available soonest? Willing to take the lowest salary? Most experienced?

Time Pressures

How quickly must the job be filled? Might a top candidate go elsewhere if we delay? What other problems might we face if the job isn't filled soon?

Resources

What can we pay? Can we afford the applicant we would most prefer to hire? What kind of person can we expect to attract for the salary we are willing to pay?

MAKING DECISIONS

Prior to and throughout the selection process, an employer must answer the above questions as well as a host of others. This requires thinking and decision making.

Thinking is a complex process. Making up your mind is never easy when the stakes are high and pressures are great to come to a quick and correct decision. To reach a conclusion a number of ingredients enter into that process: the known facts plus the decision maker's intelligence, values, needs, and emotions.

Facts Plus

Facts are statements of truth. You may be able to obtain a great many facts about a subject, but there are some facts you will never be able to get.

Do employers ever get *all* the facts about a job applicant? NO. Neither you nor any other job-seeker can possibly describe every aspect of your life, your career, your skills, and your personality in a letter, résumé, or application form.

Employers are aware of this. They know that letters and résumés are summaries designed to put an applicant in a good light.

They also know that even if they had all the facts on you, those facts could only tell what you were and what you are. That isn't good enough; what employers really want to know is *what you will be.*

"What will this applicant do for me in the future?" This is a question that cannot be answered solely on the basis of facts about that applicant's past.

Opinions

Suppose Mr. Smith advertises to fill a job opening. John Jones responds and it's his lucky day: his is the first résumé read by Smith. Does Smith immediately offer the job to Jones without reading any other application?

Don't bet on it.

Would you have any more faith in the possibility that Smith would read all the applications and then offer the job to Jones without even meeting him?

You say that's not likely to happen either? Why not? How can you tell? You don't know what was said in Jones's résumé or how it compared to what Smith wanted; you don't know if Smith is a particularly impulsive individual; you don't know if there are strong reasons to fill the job immediately; and you don't even know if the nature of the job would warrant extensive checking of candidates.

Despite this lack of knowledge, you have concluded that it would be improbable for Smith to take either of the steps posed above. Using only logic, there is no way you could have arrived at such a conclusion from the facts provided. You had to use additional information to help evaluate those facts.

Where did you get this information? From yourself. You evaluated the facts given to you by examining them in light of other information stored in your memory. You know from past experience, from experiences told to you by others, and from what you have read, that employers usually do not offer the job to the person named on the first résumé that happens to be read.

What you did was to form an opinion, based partly on the facts and partly on your experiences, of what you thought would be most likely to happen with Smith and Jones.

This is exactly the first thing that Smith would do upon reading Jones's application: form an opinion as to whether he is seriously interested in Jones.

Logic

Intelligence is the capability to think in a logical manner. Just because one *can* be logical, however, does not mean that one always *will* be logical.

One reason for this is that logic can often be applied in different ways to the same situation. Going back to our friends Smith and Jones, it would be logical for Smith to request additional information from all applicants whose initial submission leaves any questions unanswered. In the event that many people apply for the job, on the other hand, exhaustive examination of every applicant could lead to unacceptable delays in filling the job.

Employer Smith will never know whether he is misinterpreting Jones's application. He sees as completely logical an initial opinion to forget about Jones. Why? Because Smith believes that he might be in for all kinds of headaches unless he hires someone familiar with his business, and Mr. Jones, according to his own résumé, has no experience in that type of business.

Jones is only one of seventy-five others who are "questionable," whereas there are only half a dozen who look good. In Smith's mind, it would be much more logical to check out the six good prospects than to chase wild geese in the form of seventy-five questionables.

Not seeing any outstanding indications from Jones's application that Jones has unique skills or extraordinary capabilities, Smith loses interest.

Guess what? Smith's reaction makes sense. His experience has taught him that he can always go back to the questionables if none of the good prospects works out. After a couple of days, however, Smith becomes increasingly confident that he can make a good choice from the list of good prospects. As a result, Jones's résumé shortly finds itself in the circular file.

Every decision proceeds along similar lines. In the absence of a totality of facts and without a foolproof way of predicting the future, decisions always involve examining new information in the light of old information already stored in your memory.

Values

Unfortunately, facts are not the only type of information stored in a person's memory, and logic is not the only tool we use to make decisions. Values are preferences, opinions, and beliefs that have become an integral part of how a person interprets and evaluates information. Established prior to receipt of that information, values provide a built-in bias that competes with logic for control of decisions.

We each have our likes and dislikes as well as our impressions of what is good, what is bad, what is important, and what is meaningless. Some things impress us while others do not, and some people turn us on while others turn us off.

An employer may not like handwritten letters, female employees, men over forty, or applicants with a certain color skin. Are these turnoffs logical? Of course not, but you had better believe they are real. Preconceived ideas can be lodged in an employer's mind as to the need for a certain length of work experience, as to the importance of having a background in a related business, or as to the strength of character of any job applicant who is or has been out of work.

Basic Needs

Basic needs are ingrained deep within our physiological or psychological make-up as fundamental to our well-being or survival. Exerting great control over our lives, the drive to meet these needs is always instinctive and often obsessive. Someone with a particularly strong need may therefore be unable to resist the temptation to gratify that need.

Sex is one well-known need, but the sex drive does not play a big role in most hiring decisions. More often, those decisions are influenced by an employer's needs to be safe, to achieve, and to be confident in decisions.

THE NEED TO BE SAFE. This is an employer's need to be sure that hiring you will not be a mistake.

Most employers would prefer to hire people who promise modest results with zero risk rather than those who might cause serious problems in pursuit of unrealistic goals.

The need to be safe can be a very personal matter; those who are hiring may not be interested in you if they feel you are a threat to them, if you appear to be someone they could not control, or if they thought their bosses would get mad at them for hiring you.

THE NEED TO ACHIEVE. This need can be used to your advantage whenever you can help the person hiring you attain one or more personal objectives.

Can you convince people that hiring you would put more money in their pockets? Advance their careers? Relieve them of tasks they hate to do? Provide the know-how they need to reach a goal?

THE NEED TO BE CONFIDENT IN DECISIONS. A prospective boss may be perfectly confident that you can achieve results and that hiring you would represent no risks, but . . .

But what?

"What" is that you don't get the job. Why? Because of lingering doubts that haven't been erased. These might be doubts as to whether another help-wanted advertisement should be run to attract more people, about whether the next (or the last) applicant isn't in fact better than you, or that there is really a need to rush a decision.

It is impossible for anyone not confident in a decision to make that decision unless the only choice is to take the lesser of two or more evils. Rarely is that kind of emergency inherent in a hiring situation.

Without question, the need to be safe and the need to be confident in decisions are related. The difference is that the former reflects doubts about you, whereas the latter reflects someone's self-doubts at being able to make a choice.

Emotions

Anger, fear, impulsiveness, moodiness, and intuitive feelings have an enormous effect on the way we humans come to conclusions.

ANGER. Be fool enough to criticize an employer's life-style, political philosophy, religious beliefs, and so forth, and you will divert attention away from your sales pitch and make a shambles of your chances. Similar results can be achieved by showing up late for appointments, walking in unannounced and demanding an appointment, or being presumptuous.

FEAR. This emotion triggers and fuels the need to be safe. Someone may fear that you won't be able to do the job: that you won't get along with customers; that you are too old, too young, too inexperienced, too high-handed, or too good to be satisfied with the job that's open. It is also possible that you are seen by people as a threat to their own job security. In this regard, the fear of not being able to control an applicant has swayed countless hiring decisions.

IMPULSIVENESS. Jumping to conclusions is often a manifestation of a special type of fear: a fear that the decision *must* be made without delay. Impulsiveness in some people is a matter of style, with others a matter of simply panicking.

MOODINESS. Anyone not feeling well or in the midst of a troubling predicament is liable to consider your telephone or in-person presence an unwelcome annoyance. In this frame of mind, no one will be a good listener.

INTUITIVE FEELINGS. We cannot help ourselves from reacting to everything and everybody we encounter. Often unable to define what we like or dislike about other people, all we know is what we feel about them. As described here, intuitive feelings are nothing other than instinctive gut reactions.

Emotions lead to detours in the thinking process. Dwelling on unfavorable intuitive feelings, for instance, can quickly lead to rationalization of fears to justify a negative conclusion.

OUR INTERNAL COMMITTEES

Did you know that aside from various body parts and characteristics, each of us is born with an internal committee? That's right—a committee. We each think by means of a committee consisting of our personal intelligence, needs, values, and emotions.

Want to make a decision? You can't do it unless each committee member registers its vote in your mind. Whether you like it or not, all members are always there and always trying to get control of your decisions.

Even worse, other people are also always there and always trying to influence decisions. Sometimes, they have more control over your committee than you do. That's because they are good motivators. Pay attention to the following material, and you may wind up being a pretty good motivator yourself.

PERCEPTIONS INFLUENCE DECISIONS

We are each born with a certain degree of intelligence, but the way adults think and act is largely a function of their experiences, upbringing, education, social environment, and economic circumstances. These factors shape our values, needs, and emotions as well as sharpen our intelligence as a force that influences our lives.

No two people are born with the same intellectual and emotional assets, no two people have identical backgrounds, and no two people make decisions under exactly equivalent circumstances. Accordingly, no two people think alike. Each individual has a way of looking at facts and coming up with an interpretation of those facts in his or her own unique manner.

A decision that would be troublesome and risky to one person may be straightforward and secure to another. The decision-makers are different people; the circumstances are different; and the "correct" decision is different for each of them.

Truth

Aside from pure mathematics, there is rarely such a thing as an absolute truth. In hiring situations, for instance, past truths about an applicant cannot be completely identified without more facts than employers ever have. Also, there is no way anyone can predict the future truth of how previously unknown job candidates will perform.

All an employer can do is to make judgments and to form opinions as to the truth of what has happened in the past and what will probably happen in the future. These opinions, which are nothing more than educated guesses, are called *perceptions*.

As used here, a perception is an idea that is registered in your mind as an absolute truth rather than just your impression of the truth.

If for any reason people perceive that you are an unacceptable candidate, that you should not be interviewed, or that you should not be hired, you are out of the running. The truth may be that they are dead wrong. Perhaps they made a mistake; you may be the ideal person to fill the job.

Unfortunately, these are *your* truths, not the employer's. Your perceptions don't matter in these decisions; *unless an employer perceives that you are the best choice, you will not get the job!*

Similarities

Remember employer Smith and applicant Jones from earlier in this chapter? Jones lost out because he didn't have the "right" kind of career background. Why did Smith place so much emphasis on prior experience? First of all, Smith neither knows nor has the incentive to evaluate the needs, demands, or work environments in other types of businesses. He has enough trouble running his own operation without trying to relate it to another. He sees a good performer from a work environment unknown to him as a greater risk than a good performer coming from a similar environment.

Smith reasons that, compared to his needs and circumstances, applicants who have had similar jobs in similar companies in the same (or very similar) business have probably worked under similar conditions. In his opinion, it is likely that:

1. They have experienced the same on-the-job pressures they would have to live with if they worked for him.
2. They have been paid roughly the same salary he would pay for the same work.
3. They have been delegated approximately the same responsibility, authority, and latitude that he would delegate.

If these applicants seem to have a good track record, Smith is impressed. He figures that he doesn't have to spend time and money training them, he doesn't have to wait for them to get up to speed, he doesn't have to concern himself as to whether they can grasp the needs of his business, and he doesn't have to worry whether they can get results in his business. In other words, they gratify his needs to achieve *and* to be safe.

Is Smith right? Does hiring someone from a similar work environment reduce hiring risks? Don't even bother to try answering those questions. The important thing is that Smith *believes* he is right. He isn't alone, either; a large body of supervisors, managers, and business owners feel the same way.

Do you disagree with the criteria that Smith used? That and a dime will get you two nickels? Once again, your perceptions do not count.

Should you attempt to change an employer's perception of functional hiring criteria? You can try, but in most cases, you would have a better chance of convincing a lawn to mow itself.

Specificity

Take a good look at the help-wanted advertisements in any major newspaper. You will notice that surprisingly few require you to be good at the work you do.

That doesn't make any sense, does it? It does, but only from the point of view of employers who think as does our friend Smith. They know very well that they need expertise. What they are doing is defining their need for expertise in terms of someone who has a very specific work background.

Whether you first see a job specification in the help-wanted columns, at an employment agency, in the lobby outside a personnel office, or during an interview, that specification will probably be loaded with criteria describing what you should have been doing for the past few years in order for you now to be considered fully qualified.

Also included in many job specifications are educational requirements. Some jobs may have certain college degrees mandated by law, but in most cases those degrees are specified because the employer uses a degree as evidence of education and perceives that education as being necessary to do the work.

The underlying theme in these specifications is what you are and what you were. Do employers really hire people without looking at how they will perform or without trying to determine which applicant will work out best?

Of course not, but making the final hiring decision comes at the end of their search, not at the beginning. They use an applicant's history as an initial screening mechanism to weed out those candidates who they think are not qualified. Typically, those who meet the background specifications are given further consideration, while those who do not measure up are ruled out.

Some employers don't even state their criteria in help-wanted ads. Examples of this are found in help-wanted advertisements that tell you only the title of the job to be filled. Not only do people placing such ads have the same similarity perceptions as our old friend Smith, but they also perceive that a job title in one company means the same as it does in another company. They may be right, but the likelihood of their being wrong increases dramatically with the level of responsibility inherent with the job. Employers who advertise by job title may have something very specific in mind, but you'll never know what it is unless you can get to meet them.

The rarest type of job specification is results-oriented. It tells you straight out what has to be done, what results are expected, and what skills and capabilities are required. Employers who place primary emphasis on results may, however, be impressed with the "right" prior experience anyway. When you go after a job for which the ability to produce results is a major qualification, it can only help if you show you can get those results *and* that you have experience in the same business. The big difference with this type of job specification is that the employer for some reason does not want to restrict the search to only those applicants from similar businesses. This employer is asking you to brag—to show how good you are.

FIRST IMPRESSIONS

Regardless of what kind of specification an employer may be using and regardless of whether you know what's in that specification, if you do not—at first blush—seem to fit the bill, you're going to have to find another stairway.

The only exceptions are the employers who will be satisfied with "warm bodies";* someone whose needs are minimal and who does not require much in the way of skills may accept anyone who walks in off the street. For jobs that easy to get, neither the pay nor the future will probably be worth writing home about.

First impressions are deadly if they are negative because you *always* get evaluated in light of the employer's basic circumstances, including alternatives and time pressures. When other applicants look better than you on paper or sound better on the telephone, they have created a better first impression than you have. If enough good candidates apply, why would an employer pay more attention to you?

You obviously cannot control the number of other•people who apply for a job and you cannot control what they say or how they say it. But you *do* have control over what you say and how you say it.

If, when you first apply for a job, you provide information that shows that you are deficient compared to the employer's known or probable criteria, you may be accomplishing nothing but to disqualify yourself.

This is one of the big drawbacks of conventional résumés; the basic résumé format does not lend itself to providing only selective information that will be favorably received.

Warm bodies is a term used in personnel circles. The primary (and in some cases only) qualification for the job is that you must be alive at the time you start to work.

You must be selective. If anything you say could be viewed negatively, *don't say it!* Otherwise, you run a big risk of getting rejected (more about this in Chapter 7).

Your first impression is extremely strong because it is based on a little bit of facts and a whole lot of preconceived values, needs, and jumping to conclusions. Any image so formed comes largely from "information" stored deep in someone's mind. Overcoming all that prejudice can be extremely difficult—if not impossible—if that first impression is negative.

THE REAL YOU

You perceive yourself one way but others perceive you differently. Depending on who is doing the perceiving, you are liable to be one of three different people:

THE PERSON YOU PERCEIVE YOURSELF AS BEING. This is the way you see yourself. Most of us see ourselves either with too much pessimism and modesty, or with unjustified delusions of greatness.

THE PERSON OTHERS PERCEIVE YOU TO BE. This is the way others see you. Every individual in each different situation can be expected to view you in a different way.

THE PERSON YOU REALLY ARE. You are probably not objective enough to know this person. Other people can't read your mind and never have all the facts about you so they don't know the real you either.

In examining these three characters, one must conclude that the person you really are is the least important, since no one really knows that person. Granted, it is possible to get to know a person quite well over a long period of time, but employers do not have that luxury prior to hiring someone.

The person you perceive yourself as being is important, but only in the sense that you must be realistic about yourself and what you can do. If your emotions are in charge of your job search rather than your intelligence, you may be the only person on earth who believes that you can handle the job you are after.

The person others perceive you to be is by far the most important of the three. This is the only person who gets judged when you apply for a job; the only person whose statements, actions, and appearance are attributed to you; and the only person whose qualifications get factored into whether you should get a job offer.

Don't get hung up on what others *should* think about you. Pay attention to finding out what they *do* think about you, and you'll be on the right track.

THE BOTTOM LINE

It is an oversimplification to say that "It's not what you know that counts, it's who you know." In a world dominated by perceptions, it is more accurate to say that "It's not what you know that counts, it's who someone else *thinks* you know."

To get a job, the corollary is: It's not what you are that counts, it's what an employer thinks you are. Whether you are trying to make a good impression or negotiating for an offer, you must always present yourself as being exactly what the employer wants. This doesn't mean that you can lie your way to a job, but it does mean that once you learn how to control the way others perceive you, the stairways will be much easier to climb.

5. Think Like They Do

You cannot make a decision inconsistent with your own point of view. This doesn't necessarily mean that you have no regard or concern for others. It merely means that there is no way for you to make decisions other than to use *your* values, *your* needs, *your* emotions, and *your* intelligence in order to evaluate your circumstances. It is impossible, for instance, for someone else's intelligence to participate in a decision in your own mind in lieu of your own intelligence. Like breathing and eating, making up your mind is something only you can do for yourself. No one else can do it for you.

Even if someone were to put a gun to your head, you can be forced to take action contrary to your preferences only if you decide that action to be more desirable than the alternative. Your choice may not be pleasant, but it would definitely be a choice.

Employers are no different. You cannot make up or change their minds for them; you obviously cannot hope for a good working relationship by forcing or threatening them into liking you; and you cannot very well hypnotize or brainwash them.

Don't fight the way people think. Use it! Since employers rely heavily on their perceptions, you can help your cause significantly if you present yourself to them in such a way that their perceptions of you are consistent with their perceptions of the ideal candidate.

PERSONAL REACTIONS

Computers can only do what they are designed to do. Since they operate entirely on the basis of the logic programmed into their memory banks, computers are limited to the capabilities of that logic. When you "ask" a computer to do a calculation it was not programmed to perform, it will be unable to respond to your needs. Provide a computer with information it was not programmed to assimilate, and you will again get no help from the machine.

Having nothing but logic to go on, computers are smart enough to know when it makes no sense to reach conclusions and when to ask for additional information before making judgments and decisions.

Humans aren't that smart. As we have already discussed in Chapter 4, people evaluate information with tools other than facts and logic. Even when we realize that "our better judgment" is telling us to wait awhile and defer decisions until more information is available, we make judgments anyway. Our values, needs, and emotions push and tug at us to react, to decide, and to do it *now*.

Human beings are incapable of receiving information without reacting to it. When provided with facts and statements, we instinctively ask: What does this mean to me? Should I do anything about it? Is it good or bad for me? What does my experience tell me about it? Does it represent a risk to me? How can I use it to my advantage? We may ask other questions as well, but regardless of the circumstances and regardless of the nature or type of information with which we are confronted, the result, without exception, is a reaction and one or more conclusions. We may conclude that information is meaningless or critical, that we should or should not act on it, or that it annoys or pleases us. But we *will* draw a conclusion; we can't help it.

Employers always draw conclusions from the information provided to them by job applicants. What you have to do is to see to it that they draw only those conclusions you want drawn.

MAKING STATEMENTS

If you had a well-known reputation for honesty and recognized skill in getting things done, employers would have positive preconceived ideas about the integrity of your word and the meaning of your confidence in being able to do a job. You would also have no difficulty in finding work.

As things are, employers place great weight on their own sense of values and with no prior knowledge of you or your work, they have no reason to place high value on what you say. Merely stating that you are good doesn't make it true, at least not in an employer's eyes.

But if you can motivate that employer to *perceive* that you are good, you are making progress. Remember: we act on perceptions as if they were absolute truths! Conclusions drawn by an employer on the basis of perceptions have enormous influence over his or her thinking, whereas your opinions as a perfect stranger have very little influence.

Stating that you are qualified for a job is likely to result in the employer concluding that you have some degree of self-confidence. That's okay, but if you come on too strong, it might be concluded that you are arrogant. That's not okay.

In any case, why settle for okay when you can do better?

DISTORTING THE TRUTH

Given the strength of perceptions in decision-making, it stands to reason that the manner in which facts are presented is as important, if not more important, than the facts themselves.

TRUE FACT 1. Lisa is a graduate mechanical engineer.

TRUE FACT 2. Lisa has four years' experience in industry.

TRUE FACT 3. Lisa has recently established and implemented a system that resulted in a 75 percent decrease in energy usage costs.

So Lisa applies for a job as a project engineer and includes the above information in a letter of application. The employer reads that letter and immediately goes into overdrive drawing conclusions:

1. She has the right education.
2. She has the right experience.
3. She gets results.
4. She is knowledgeable about energy analyses.
5. She is cost conscious.

Is she? Does she? On the basis only of the facts provided above, you simply don't know. Perhaps she worked in a large office with her desk in one corner. The office had no heat but plenty of windows and four ceiling lights, each with its own switch. Maybe she decided that there was no need to light up the whole place and turned off the switches for the three fixtures not near her desk. Isn't that a "75 percent decrease in energy usage costs"? You bet it is!

By now you also may be drawing conclusions about Lisa's character and integrity. If that's what you are doing, go back and read what was said about her. You can draw negative conclusions about what she did only by getting hung up on the discussion of what she may have done. If you use your intelligence rather than your impulsiveness, you will realize that you have drawn conclusions you had no grounds for drawing.

You have to remember that you are examining Lisa's application in the midst of studying a book describing the importance of perceptions and illustrating the fact that logic plays a small role in many decisions. An employer, on the other hand, would probably examine her letter in the midst of a busy work day at a desk loaded with work perhaps including mail from several other job applicants. Unless you insult an employer's intelligence by stating facts that lead to preposterous conclusions, a hasty look made during the crush of business may result in his or her jumping to just the conclusion you want reached. It is therefore reasonable to assume that some employers, on the basis of the facts provided earlier, will conclude that Lisa is a competent, experienced engineer.

Claiming to be an energy expert because you know how to turn off light switches is obviously an extreme example of how it is possible—without lying—to distort facts to suit your own purposes and how—on face value—you really can't tell the difference between a distorted fact and an absolute truth.

It is also a good example of how events and situations take on entirely different meanings depending on how they are presented and described.

IMPLICATIONS

An implication can be defined as information that you present in a manner as to motivate an employer to draw a specific conclusion. Not just any conclusion, but one that you have predetermined will help you to get interviewed or hired.

Lisa, by stating the facts the way she did, neither drew nor stated opinions or conclusions, but she did make a number of implications. Aside from the biggie on energy savings, another implication involves the industry in which she has worked for four years. What industry? You don't know. What was she doing in that industry? You don't know that either, but sandwiched in between mention of an engineering degree and an achievement that sounds technological, many employers would conclude that she worked as an engineer in energy-related fields.

What Lisa did or did not do is unimportant here. The important thing is that the way she has stated the facts, reading her letter would, if it didn't impress you, at least have a good chance of leading you to conclude that you should find out more about the truth of Lisa's qualifications.

Admit it—aren't you the least bit curious?

That's exactly the point. Lisa *wants* employers to be curious. She's already completed Step 2 of the employment process (communication with the employer) and now her letter is working on Step 3 (make a good first impression). She merely wants to whet the employer's appetite for more information about her.

ASSOCIATIONS AND PERCEPTIONS

One reason implications work is that we tend to associate information given to us with perceptions we have formed previously. As soon as you saw the name "Lisa," you undoubtedly concluded that we were talking about a woman, but no mention of gender was made in any of the three facts given about Lisa. Not until the employer started concluding did Lisa get referred to as a "she." Without question, it is highly unlikely that anyone named Lisa would be male, but presuming Lisa to be female is strictly a perception, an educated guess based on experience rather than on hard facts.

Another association in Lisa's case was energy-saving systems with engineering expertise rather than with simple common sense. The same phenomenon would control if you tell an employer that you graduated from a prestigious college or that you worked at a highly respected firm. The well-known high standards of your alma mater or previous employer, by implication, become associated with you in the mind of the employer.

GETTING THE MOST FROM YOUR STRENGTHS

If you didn't like the energy-expert implication, how about saying that you were a Municipal Transportation Coordinator when in fact you were a volunteer guard at school crossings? You could even claim to be an Environmental Control Director because you drove a garbage truck. Aside from offending your sense of scruples, however, getting carried away with implications may give you a bad case of foot-in-mouth disease at interview time.

There are many ways in which you can take advantage of implications without going overboard. Take a good look at the following sentence. Presuming for the moment that it applied to you, it would help to make a very good impression while being completely straightforward and truthful.

> Promoted four years ago to my present job as Furniture Manufacturing Manager, I initiated programs that met objectives by increasing productivity 23 percent while cutting labor costs 12 percent.

Only twenty-nine words, but look at how much they imply:

- That you are reasonably stable. You have been with your current employer for four years as Production Manager plus an unspecified time before you were promoted. You are therefore someone who is not apt to jump around.

- That you are what is called a self-starter—someone who initiates programs without having to be told what to do every step of the way.

- That you are output conscious, an absolute must for a Manufacturing Manager.

- That you are cost conscious, a helpful trait for anyone looking for a new job.

- That you know how to get impressive results.

- That you are in charge of manufacturing furniture where you work now.

- That you operate according to management-by-objectives. By mentioning programs and objectives, you imply that you are organized.

- That you understand the needs of the furniture business. To another furniture manufacturer this implies that you would not have to "learn the ropes."

- That you have experience managing people (you couldn't very well reduce labor costs unless you had people to manage).

- That you were well thought of when you were promoted four years ago. Presuming that your accomplishments are as you state them to be, it might also be implied that you are still well thought of, but this is stretching things.

- That you are probably in your late thirties, give or take a few years. People who get promoted to top-management jobs tend to do so after ten to fifteen years experience, not four years or forty years. This implication of your age also implies that you have plenty of fruitful years ahead.

- That being employed, you are not desperate to grasp at any job offer that comes along.

Here we started out with a short sentence with no distortions and no stretching of the truth, and yet twelve implications could be made. That being the case, twelve conclusions could be reached by employers. Did you state that you were a stable person? Did you say that you were organized, or that you were almost forty years old?

You did not. You said none of those things and you expressed no opinions whatsoever. By coming across as factual, rather than pushy, and by providing a concentration of the type of facts that employers like to see, you would impress a number of prospective bosses simply by allowing them to reach conclusions to their hearts' content.

Wait a minute! Where did you say that you were factual rather than pushy? You didn't, but the way you wrote the sentence *did* say it. Make that thirteen implications.

Want to try for fourteen? It's possible that although you are currently employed, you don't expect to be employed for long. Maybe your company was sold or merged with another in a way that has eliminated your job effective three months from now. Maybe you just lost your job effective two weeks from now. Because you said that your "present" job was Furniture Manufacturing Manager, you imply, by not discussing your future prospects on that job, that it will continue at your discretion. There is no reason for the reader to suspect otherwise.

That's not all. One implication that you were really sneaky about relates to job titles. Titles have all kinds of meanings depending on where you are working.

At one corporation, a Vice-President of Production Control may oversee all phases of purchasing, raw material processing, manufacturing, scheduling, packaging, and shipping, with a manager reporting to him in each of those areas. Yet across town, there may be another company of approximately the same size and in the same business. This company doesn't have any vice-presidents and the production operation is headed up by someone with the title of Manufacturing Manager.

You certainly wouldn't want to lie about your title, but what are you trying to imply when you list a title? Were you really the number-one person in manufacturing management?

Believe it or not, there is a sixteenth. If your application said nothing more than the twenty-nine words we are talking about, you would say something else about your professionalism, your neatness, and your attention to detail by sending in a properly spelled, correctly addressed, and neatly typed letter.

IMPACT

Great, so you can get sixteen implications out of twenty-nine words. So what? Is an employer going to examine your application word by word like we're doing here? If not, will those sixteen implications result in sixteen positive conclusions or will several be missed?

Who knows? There are no guarantees, and maybe only half the implications are picked up by the employers to whom you apply. But is that one sentence the only one you would include in your application?

Certainly not! You could easily put a half dozen more sentences no longer than that in a short letter typed on one side of one sheet of standard-size business stationery. Let's see. If you could cram sixteen implications into each of those sentences, you would have a total of 102 things to say about yourself on a document that could be read in a matter of seconds. Even if your batting average is one conclusion reached out of every two you wanted to be reached, fifty-one positive conclusions drawn about you in less than a minute ain't bad. As a matter of fact, it's probably enough to make a good first impression. Isn't that what you wanted?

Don't worry if your background does not include management jobs with impressive titles. There are a number of different ways you can use to generate quite truthful statements about yourself that will make good impressions on prospective "customers." You will learn how in Part B.

You may not be able to get one implication for every two words. Perhaps you will in most cases be able to get one for every three or four words. The trick is not to play games with sentence structure, but rather to make every word count and to make every punctuation mark, every phrase, and every clause work as hard for you as possible so you can make the greatest possible impact in the shortest possible time.

Why is time so important? The people evaluating your applications have a great deal to do other than to read the mail you send in. If you don't grab their attention and interest right away, they have no incentive to pay further attention to you, particularly when they have also heard from other applicants who instantly made a good impression. This is exactly what happened to applicant Jones back in Chapter 4.

By the way, there is a name for the conclusions reached as a result of implications: *inferences.* Chapter 11 is devoted entirely to how you can say things in different ways to create favorable inferences.

Audible Implications

What can you do at face-to-face or in telephone interviews? When you write you can revise your words and sentences for days until you have your implications perfect, but when you are talking to someone, your answers as well as your questions must be on the tip of your tongue, ready when needed.

But you *can* revise and re-revise what you say at interviews. You can't do it during an interview without sounding ridiculous, but you can rehearse and you can make up, as discussed in Chapter 3, a series of contingency plans for use in interviews so that you can perfect your techniques.

The biggest difference between written and audible implications is that what you say in writing can be read over and over again, but what has missed someone's ear the first time will never be heard again unless you say it again. Should a conversation be interrupted for any reason, pick up at a point *before* the interruption so you will not lose any continuity of thought on the part of the employer.

People may not be able to comprehend what you are implying as fast as you can speak. When you are talking, your listener may still be digesting what you said several seconds ago. If you talk too fast or change subjects too quickly, it may not be possible to keep up with what you are saying. As a consequence, a portion of your message will be wasted. The twenty-nine word sentence from the Furniture Manufacturing Manager, for instance, would—if spoken—be easier to comprehend if broken into four separate sentences:

> I was promoted four years ago to my present job as Furniture Manufacturing Manager. Since then, I've initiated a number of programs and, frankly, they've all met objectives. One, for example, was instrumental in increasing productivity by 23 percent. Another decreased direct labor costs by 12 percent.

This is almost double the number of words used in writing the same information, but delivered in a natural manner that provides the facts in a natural sequence and that allows the employer to reach the right conclusions as a result of what appears to be a logical cause-and-effect relationship. The cause? Your skills and capabilities. The effect? The results you tell about. The implication? That those results were entirely a direct result of your expertise and that you can get the same results elsewhere.

Optical Implications

Picture a man wearing an expensive, well-tailored suit. He has an erect posture and an elegant manner. Would he best fit your image of a ditchdigger, a banker, or a derelict? How about a muscular man in jeans, tee-shirt, and hard hat? Or would you prefer to answer with respect to a gentleman who reeks of booze and looks as if he has slept in the same clothes for three months?

Your choices are not difficult. If the image of a person fits your preconceived idea of what that person should look like, you are comfortable with both the person and the image. Were the gent in the hard hat to tell you that he is the banker, however, you would be dubious. If the drunk purported to be in the money business, you would simply not believe it.

What would be the reaction of a bank president who is greeted by a prospective executive wearing jeans, tee-shirt, and hard hat? Certainly not one of approval.

Perhaps that's an extreme example, but how about people who show up with hair uncombed, clothes wrinkled, fingernails dirty, and so on. What image are they trying to match? That of a person who is sloppy and somewhat disorganized?

You imply a great deal about yourself by the way you look. It is relatively easy to "look the part" for a job you want—in some cases it is easier than meeting some of the employer's qualifications. If it's too much trouble for you to look good at interviews, employers may conclude that you are lazy. They may also conclude that they should hire someone else.

6. P Is for Personality

After an extensive search for talent, the owner of Coalburning Wristwatches, Inc., settles on two applicants as being the best candidates to fill the post of a Marketer who can convince people to buy watches powered by a tiny coal furnace built into the watch. Both candidates have about the same length of experience in the watch business, both come highly recommended by wholesalers and other industry specialists, and both have a clear record of accomplishments.

One candidate, Al, is an analytical person who tends to be pragmatic and never hesitates to speak his mind: "If anybody can do this, I can. The only request I have is that we realize that people have to get used to the idea that a coal-burning wristwatch is safe and practical. But don't worry . . . with my advertising programs and a little luck, the buying public will become believers in only a few months."

The other candidate, Ed, has a different style. Ed is the picture of outward optimism: "This wristwatch is the greatest thing since sliced bread," he tells the owner of the company. "I'll bury your production people with business."

Which one would you prefer?

Realistically, your selection would depend on your style of operating and how much you believe in the potential of coal-fired personal timepieces. Were you to feel that the idea was interesting, yet a long shot as a big-selling item, you might very well prefer someone like Al, who would be more apt to take a measured approach that would not pour effort and money into promoting a product if it became obvious that it wouldn't sell.

If, on the other hand, you had spent the last ten years of your life perfecting that wristwatch, it would be your baby and the last thing you would want to hear is that there would be potential problems and that luck and fancy advertising programs would be required to sell your wonderful idea. You would definitely go for Ed, thinking that he would be off and running for sales while Al was still analyzing his way out of negative thinking.

The person who would be hired to promote those wristwatches would get selected on the basis of how his personality blended with that of whoever makes the hiring decision. If the blend is good, the employer can realistically conclude that he and the new employee will be able to work well together. With a combination that won't mix, however, an employer would be asking for trouble by hiring someone he didn't like or someone he didn't think he could get along with.

This aspect of getting a job is very much like mixing two chemicals together in a large vat. Combinations like oil and water will stay mixed only when frequently shaken up. No boss will want to have to shake you up regularly. If you don't blend in, an employer will need you about as much as a moose needs a hatrack.

JOB COMPATIBILITY

You might think a coal-burning wristwatch to be a ridiculous idea, but who knows? Maybe there's a way to make one work.

Selecting employees on the basis of personality is a different story. Far from being ridiculous, it represents a great deal of intelligence on the part of employers. They know that regardless of what skills you have, unless your personality is compatible with the job and with the people with whom you have to work, you won't last.

As an example, a construction foreman would be expected to have a personality quite unlike that of a kindergarten teacher, whereas both would be quite different from a stockbroker. Similarly, top-level managers and career file clerks will have attitudinal and other characteristics that are dissimilar relative to their job, their outlook, their commitment to their work, and their loyalty to their employer.

Method of compensation, location, and scope of responsibility may also require different personality types:

- Some sales people prefer the excitement and higher income possibilities inherent with being paid strictly on commissions, whereas others are not comfortable unless they have the security of a regular paycheck.

- One secretary may be perfectly at ease handling the typing for six or seven executives while another, who is an even better typist, might not be able to handle the conflicting and hectic nature of priorities assigned by multiple bosses.

- Applicants who have lived all their lives in big cities might be unhappy taking a job a hundred miles from the nearest metropolis.

Note that *personality* means more than your outward style in dealing with life. A more complete meaning of the word is that it defines the traits, habits, and mannerisms that are unique to you. In this regard, none of the personality differences discussed above is good or bad, just different from one another. The differences are also representative of the fact that varying fields and activities require varying personalities to cope with and meet the demands of each job. This is another reason why employers like similar prior experience: it provides them with justification for perceiving that you have not only the right skills, but also the right personality.

PEOPLE COMPATIBILITY

People compatibility is a fancy way to describe your ability to get along with others in a specific job environment. If you get a job, not only will you have to get along with the people who already work there, but you may well also be required to get along with customers and other outside people.

One example of the importance of people compatibility can be illustrated by taking a look at a "New York" salesman. In the Big Apple, the fast-talking, let's-get-to-the-point hard sell is commonplace and often successful. In rural South Carolina, however, that sales approach would be a disaster, as would the chances of a New Yorker who knew no other way to sell.

INTERVIEWER/BOSS COMPATIBILITY

Your first interview may not be with the person who would be your boss. Employment agency people and personnel managers might have to come first. Not only do you have to impress each of those people, you also have to convince them that you have what they perceive to be the boss's perception of the right personality for the job and for the people with whom you would have to work.

This remote-control evaluation can lead you to waste an opportunity if you give the personnel manager a chance to reject you because he didn't like you or because he felt that you wouldn't be compatible with the boss. Being rejected by anyone other than the person to whom you would report is a waste because the *only* person who really knows how the boss will relate to your personality is the boss himself and even he won't know until after meeting you.

PERFECTION

From a personality standpoint, achieving perfect compatibility with someone requires the other person to:

- like you
- respect you
- trust you
- feel that you meet his or her basic needs in terms of relating to other people

Occasionally, you can achieve perfect compatibility with someone else, perhaps even with several people at the same time. To convince people that you are compatible with them, however, generally takes some time, during which you can get to know each other's needs and values. In a male–female social setting, this is accomplished through dating and courtship, and despite long premarital relationships, some couples find out the hard way that they are not compatible at all.

It's far worse in an interview setting, where at most you have a couple of hours to size up the interviewer, correctly assess his or her needs and values, and act in a way that is in your best interests, all the while being grilled about your background.

Neither this nor any other book will be able to quickly make you an expert at figuring out what people like, what their needs are, and what you have to do to convince them that you are compatible with them. You *can* learn how to do this, but it takes a great deal of time and practice, and you certainly cannot pull out a book in the middle of a conversation in order to figure out what to do next.

Unless you are already pretty good at sizing up others and acting accordingly, don't try making on-the-spot alterations to your personality; you may appear too obvious or put on the wrong act and make things worse than they should be. The main factor you have going for you is that you do *not* need perfect compatibility to get a job. You're not going to marry the boss, you just want to work for him. From a personality standpoint, the interviewer/boss doesn't have to love you and, since we are talking about what is primarily a business environment, he doesn't even have to like you a great deal. As long as he does not dislike you and intuitively sees no reason why you couldn't function together, you'll do okay.

Not being disliked requires you to avoid displaying strong personality traits. Be businesslike, courteous, matter-of-fact, and, if you tend to have a "big" personality, don't show it in applications and don't bring it to interviews. This way, you don't give the employer much with which to find fault. The only exception to this would occur if you determined during the course of an interview that a certain type personality is highly valued by the employer. If you can, show that you are that type or can be it when necessary.

Respect and trust are necessary, but these can be achieved to a sufficient degree by telling a plausible story in a straightforward manner. More on this in Part B.

RELATIONSHIP NEEDS

Did you ever work for a boss who simply would not delegate any significant level of responsibility to anyone? With that type of boss, you are looked upon with horror if you show that you are a self-starter who can operate with a minimum of supervision. Or, a boss may be so egotistical that he cannot imagine his employees making the right decision without his help.

Reluctance to delegate has, in the great majority of instances, nothing whatsoever to do with the gravity of the situation and nothing to do with the competence of the employee. It has everything to do with the employer not feeling comfortable unless he is controlling every action of every person in the company at every step of the way.

Other employers have different needs. Some can relate to you only by being an overbearing bully, others may be so uncomfortable in dealing with people that you'll never get a clear understanding of how they think you are doing, and still others will delegate everything to you, but won't take the time or trouble to give you direction or help you solve sticky problems. In addition, some employers have a need to engage in participative management so they can gain from your ideas, whereas others don't really care what you think. (Unless they come up with an idea of their own, it's a worthless idea!)

There is nothing particularly intelligent or rational about some of these management styles. They are not used because of the intellectual powers of the people who use them but rather because each of us has a style all our own in dealing with others. Your style may make no sense to anyone else, but it's the only way you feel comfortable working with people. You may be very political in terms of office politics, you may be very independent and strong-willed, you may be arrogant, you may be easygoing, and you may be indifferent. Like the management types described above, you act the way you do because of basic needs that you could not gratify if you acted any other way.

Isn't it great? People act the way their inner drives compel them to act and we're all happy. Right?

Wrong. Unless the people in an organization can make it their business to get along with each other, everybody doing his or her own thing would lead to arguments without end, fighting, and anarchy. Again, you don't have to be in love with the people you work for, but if you can't coexist and get the job done, you have no business working together. Fortunately, most of us are not so rigid that we can't adapt as necessary to get along with bosses and co-workers.

In a hiring situation, needs to relate to employees in certain ways are generally expressed in the broader *need to be safe*, as described in Chapter 4.

CHALLENGES

A tyrannical supervisor may or may not be fully aware of the impact of his or her personality and management style on the people in the organization. The supervisor may honestly believe that he is a prudent and reasonable executive who is quite easy to work for.

He may, on the other hand, be fully aware of the fact that he tends to terrorize people, and he may be concerned that weak subordinates may tell him only what he likes to hear, resulting in his getting a rather biased indication of what is happening. Consequently, he will seek out strong-willed employees who will have the courage to tell him the truth, no matter how bad it is.

Then there is a third type of tyrant: one who absolutely will not tolerate any independence of thought or action. You'll never be able to get along with this boss unless you always agree with him and follow his instructions unquestioningly. A forceful individual working for this type tyrant will surely cause much in the way of office fireworks.*

Theoretically, your primary challenge in an interview with a prospective boss is to find out what kind of personality he really has, whether it is compatible with yours, and how he would define compatibility. In the case of a tyrant, you would have to determine which of the above three variations best described him.

Unfortunately, it is unlikely that you'll be able to find out that much about anyone in an hour or two. An interview is a best-foot-forward situation during which people are on their best behavior. The circumstances are quite different from what goes on during a hectic workday. As a result, you and the interviewer are not going to act nearly the same as you would if you knew each other very well and were trying to meet a common goal. During an interview, however, you may each be trying to outfox the other and, to at least some extent, putting on an act to make a good impression.

You've got to be very, very good at dealing with people to go through this process, determine what it takes to make a stranger feel that you are compatible, and then "put on" just the right personality to make him feel that you meet his relationship needs.

You may not be experienced or comfortable at doing that, but don't worry; you can deal with meeting needs the same way you deal with being liked. Just keep your personality under wraps until you know more about what you have to do to make the employer feel comfortable with you. Your real challenge will be to draw out the interviewer into conversation that will reveal his true personality. Techniques for doing that are discussed in Chapter 13.

---

*With apologies to the tyrants of the world, there is no intention here to pick on such people. Their ways of running things are often quite productive, if not exciting. They are singled out only because they tend to be so extreme that their characteristics are often easy to recognize.

BE APPROPRIATE

Stop to think about it and you will realize that the simplest procedures are often the most effective and easiest to apply. This is certainly true when it comes to selling yourself in terms of your personality.

Be appropriate. Dress for the job you want, display a personality that is consistent with that job, and take care to do everything you can to make it impossible for employers to perceive that you are incompatible with their jobs, their people, their customers, or their own personalities.

7. Measuring Up to Their Standards

The functional hiring criteria are the objectives inherent in the circumstances (see Chapter 4) under which the job is being filled. You may see these criteria in any or all of these forms:

- A function description of what has to be done and what skills are required. The function may be implied simply by job title.
- The expected results. In some situations, potential may be more important than related business experience.
- Related background criteria in terms of education, experience, and knowledge of the business. As shown in Chapter 4, these criteria are often used to weed out supposedly unqualified candidates.
- Applicable personal criteria. Someone in sales, for instance, must have the right personality, the right ability to articulate, and the right appearance. (Personal criteria in terms of functional hiring requirements are not related to the employer liking or disliking you but rather to what he believes is necessary to do the job.)

You may not be aware of all of an employer's functional hiring criteria, but if you pay close attention to the following pages and chapters, you should be able to estimate those criteria quite well.

The Hidden Hiring Criteria

The *functional* hiring criteria are the qualifications that get put into ads and job specifications, but they are by no means the only ones that you will have to measure up to. *Hidden* criteria have nothing to do with your ability to perform, get results, or to do the job. They are related to the employer's personal likes and dislikes, personality, and drives.

If an employer doesn't want anyone above a certain age, won't hire people with skin color other than his own, or refuses to employ women, those criteria are never stated or put in writing. Discrimination on the basis of age, sex, or race is illegal, yet it happens. Some employers have preconceptions they simply must live by, but they're not stupid enough to make their hiring practices public knowledge.

Even worse, many people are not fully aware of the extent to which their hiring decisions are controlled by strongly driven needs, values, and emotions. Their hidden criteria may be entirely subconscious until triggered by something you do or say—or even by your appearance, your taste in clothes, or the way you act.

Good examples of hidden criteria can be found by looking at the ways different personalities react with one another. Do you really think a boss would run an ad for someone who "must be pliable enough to be easily dominated by my dictatorial way of running this place"? You'll meet this kind of boss, but don't hold your breath waiting to see his personality preferences expressed in writing.

Would an employer say (or even realize) that he or she prefers "employees who always agree with me, regardless of how wrong I might be"? No, and yet you undoubtedly have worked for or known a number of characters who can't stand being contradicted.

How about a criterion that specified a need for a "personality compatible with mine"? That requirement never gets stated either, but it is quite obviously always an integral part of the final selection.

To most employers, the very concept of making hiring decisions based on criteria that have nothing to do with performance is ridiculous. *They* would never do that.

It's difficult (often impossible) to tell when this is happening to you, because the employer may not even realize what it is that is bothering him about you. He "knows" only that you're not making a good impression. But he doesn't know this because of his intelligence; it's his intuitions that are controlling, spurred on by a negative reaction to preconceived values. Before long, rationalization will take over and he will come up with a reason for not hiring you.

The big problem with the hidden criteria is that you don't know what they are. You don't even know whether they are conscious or subconscious, but you can bet your bottom dollar that there *are* hidden criteria associated with every job.

Handling hidden criteria requires you to avoid generalizations; these criteria are unique to the individual employer and can only be dealt with one person at a time. Presuming that one employer has the same hidden criteria as another could be quite erroneous. In addition, you must also realize that you may never know *all* of the hidden criteria that may be buried in someone's mind; the best you can do is to get an employer to talk at length with you about the job and his or her thoughts on how the job should be performed. This is accomplished by asking questions that require the other person to respond in narrative form rather than with a simple "yes" or "no" answer.

As an example, presume you are a whiz at credit collections. To bring this out, you might ask an employer: "Are collections a problem for your accounting people?" and get a curt yes or no that tells you nothing. But if you ask: "Typically, could you tell me some of the more nagging problems your accounting people run up against in this business?" there's no way you can get a one-word answer. What you will get is information on what is important to that employer and possibly also some feel for what kind of personality he would find preferable.

After listening to the answer, if you still don't find the opening you wanted, you might say "That's fascinating, but I'm surprised you didn't mention collections." Again, you haven't left room for a one-word answer and again, you get more information.

The more questions you ask, the more you can find out about the hidden criteria; if you had the sense to memorize a few good questions before an interview starts, so much the better.

You'll learn more about questioning and ferreting out criteria in Chapter 13. For the most part, intelligence takes a holiday when hidden criteria are used against you. Biases, deep-rooted fears, needs to associate with (or avoid) certain personality types, and all kinds of groundless intuitions and rationalizations run rampant as you are evaluated.

Don't let *your* intelligence take a holiday; someone should be in logical control of the way you are judged when you apply for jobs and when you are interviewed. If you're smart, that someone will be you.

RECOGNIZING HIRING CRITERIA

Okay, what *does* the employer want? Any or all of twelve criteria clues may be expressed or implied in a help-wanted advertisement:

1. The title of the job.
2. The title of the person to whom you would report.
3. Educational requirements.
4. Functional personal characteristics.
5. Experience requirements.
6. Skills required.
7. Functions to be performed.
8. Results expected.
9. Employer's name.
10. Employer's location.
11. Classification of employer's customers or users.
12. Unique characteristics of the job (heavy travel, odd hours, etc.).

The more of these clues that you see in an ad, the more you know about the employer's functional criteria and the better position you are in to provide, as an integral part of your application, similarities between what you are or what you have done and what the employer wants. The more similarities you can show, the better your chances will be of making a good impression. This, of course, is what similarities are all about: you first figure out what the employer is looking for, and then you show that *you* are the person who has it.

Unfortunately, most ads really don't tell you a great deal, but even a small amount of information can be extremely valuable. If all you know is the job title, fine. What does that title imply in terms of required skills, functions, and expected results?

Job title plus the name of a business or industry gives you even more clues. Even when they don't say so, employers who name their industry will generally consider knowledge of their industry a plus.

How about the employer's name and location? Can you see what clues that information provides? With an employer's identity, you can do some research on the size, business, and customers of the company and, in many cases, the names of their key people. If yours is an executive job, it may help to know if the company is run by its founder, whether it is family owned, and what the ages are of the people in charge. You may not find all of these goodies in the ad, but Chapter 9 will show you how you can research most of the rest. Location, by the way, is a clue also in that employers may tend to prefer people who are nearby, available on short notice, and don't have to relocate to take the job.

Don't overlook the descriptive terms used in ads. *Senior manager, multinational sales, executive secretary, creative individuals, high-level professionals,* and *management specialist* are expressions that contain clues. *Recent grad* is also a clue that the employer doesn't want a lot of experience and won't pay a great deal of money. *Mature* on the other hand, probably means "very experienced." Can you show similarities relative to clues such as these?

Ads, of course, are not the only source for job potentials. You may apply to firms that haven't advertised and if they have an opening, you may get a favorable response. It is hoped that you will already have applied the instructions in Chapter 3, and you have some reason to believe what you have to offer would be of interest to them.

With unsolicited applications, you know the company name and location and industry. You also know or can look up its size. You know the job you want so you should be able to come up with a generic title for that job as well as the skills and typical personality type required, the functions to be performed, and the types of results expected. You should also be able to make a pretty good stab at the title of the person to whom you would report. Lots of clues here too!

The objective in recognizing job criteria is *not* to go bananas finding hidden meanings in every word or phrase of a help-wanted ad. Should you find yourself getting paranoid about these ads and job specifications, you'll never make progress.

What you should do is to operate on the basis of probabilities interpreted by simple common sense. Employers don't go out of their way to build secret meanings into their words, and they certainly don't read your applications and interpret your conversations as if their entire decision hinged on a word here and a word there.

TAILOR-MADE FOR THE JOB

Anticipating employer interests is a matter of telling them what they want to hear. As we have already established, employers tend to be highly specific about what they want, and no two of them think exactly alike. Combined with the fact that they hire on the basis of their own selfish interests, you can be certain that a sales pitch that impresses one employer may be met with scorn by another, even if they are both in the same business.

Tailoring means that you have to constantly remind yourself that you can't afford to think in terms of what "they" want. "They" is plural, and you *must* tailor every application to the specific individual who will be reading your letter or speaking to you. You have to ask "What does *he* want?" "What will impress *her*?"

Whether you use letters, résumés, telephone calls, or walk-in visits, sending the same message to every potential employer will make it all the more difficult to impress the maximum number of prospects. To best sell yourself, you have to use similarities to make each "customer" feel as if you are a *perfect* fit to his particular needs; and that what he has to offer represents a perfect fit to the work, salary, and opportunities you seek. If you have to make every application unique and different from every other, so be it. Tailoring is a small price to pay for saving a great deal of time and trouble.

Tailoring requires you to treat each prospect as a separate and distinct person with unique needs. Not only does tailoring help by restricting you to topics that will create a good impression, it also forces you to show the courtesy to not waste an employer's time by talking about matters he considers insignificant.

The primary benefit of tailoring is that it requires you to direct your application toward the key points most likely to be on the employer's mind. If you can state the right experience, illustrate the right capabilities, and list the right education, there is no need for the employer to question your qualifications in those areas; you start out on a positive note before doubts even arise.

Appeal to Their Basic Needs

Applying for a job can be like leaving the cookie jar in plain sight of a little boy; the employer won't be able to resist the temptation to partake of the treats before his eyes. You don't have to tell little boys to take cookies from the jar, and you certainly don't have to force them to do so either. All you have to do is to make it easy for them to see and reach into the jar.

Provide plenty of opportunities to meet the employer's needs to achieve and to be safe. Present yourself as someone who is a proven performer and who will cause no problems if hired. The employer must believe that you will get the results he wants without any risks whatsoever.

To "provide opportunities" is not the same as to force-feed. Keep in mind that employers will believe only what they personally conclude, not what you say they should believe. You must therefore use examples of outstanding results, reliability, experience, and expertise to create implications that will cause employers to conclude—on their own—that you are the perfect person to meet their needs to achieve and be safe. When you have a good feel for an employer's basic needs relative to his or her personality type, you will be in a position—if you can—to offer that type, using implications that make your "cookie jar" irresistible.

Recognize the Employer's Circumstances

Look for whom is doing the hiring and where he or she fits into the organization. Will that person have something to gain personally from your being hired? As an example, a company may be in business to make a profit, but an office manager's career may live or die on the basis of a secretary's ability to be productive. Similarly, the boss of a very large company might be concerned solely with your impact on profitability, whereas the personnel manager would have to also be interested in how you would get along with the people already on board. In a smaller company, however, the top honcho might get more involved in personnel considerations directly.

Recognizing the employer's circumstances also puts you in a better position to understand what chain of command he or she has to go through to approve hiring decisions; it might also provide you with insight into what risks the person fears most and what criteria you have to deal with.

NEGATIVES

Hiring is a process of elimination. Out of hundreds who apply, typically about a dozen are selected as being worth interviewing. Out of that dozen, perhaps only two or three are interviewed a second time, and only one of them is chosen to be the person to whom an offer is extended.

You might have fewer positive attributes than another candidate, but if you also have fewer negatives, you just might be the more attractive applicant. For you to get the offer, you must still be making favorable impressions after everyone else has been rejected. Not only do you have to make a good first impression, you must continue to make good impressions throughout every step in the path to a job. It may take no more than one negative factor to derail your candidacy, so you cannot afford to do or say anything that might go against you.

When in Doubt, Leave it Out

To avoid being rejected, you have to avoid making a bad impression. This is unfortunately not quite the same as making a good impression. The difference is in the context in which statements are made and interpreted. The two following sentences are an interesting example of perfectly innocent information that will absolutely kill your job chances if used in the wrong situations:

> A 1981 honors graduate of Harvard College, I have a Master's degree in Business Administration.

> A 1961 honors graduate of Harvard College, I have a Master's degree in Business Administration.

Each statement implies a well-educated person, with above-average intelligence, who was able to perform in an exemplary manner at a top school attended by high-caliber people. Those are good implications.

Beyond those, the difference of twenty years in graduating dates also implies a difference of twenty years in age. Greater age in turn implies more maturity, more experience, better development of skills, and more potential for commitment (the older person would be more likely to have family and fiscal responsibilities that would discourage whimsical job changes). Those are also good implications.

On the negative side, greater age implies higher salary requirements, more resistance to learning new ways, less enthusiasm (and less energy) for long hours, and more tendency to seek security rather than advancement. These implications are not so good.

Whether any implication is good or bad depends upon what the employer wants. A firm seeking someone who does not command top salary may be leery of talking to a seasoned executive whose salary requirements would likely be beyond their budget, whereas an employer looking for experience would be suspicious of the capabilities of a recent graduate.

Unless you know with a reasonable degree of certainty that some information will help, don't use it. You can say "An honors graduate of Harvard College, I have a Master's degree in Business Administration." No year, no bad implications, no negatives, and yet you are still left with positive implications. Should you come across a situation in which stating the year will work to your advantage, add it.

As shown by this next example, age is not the only type of information that can hurt when needlessly volunteered.

> Working part time for a small precious metals dealer, I once sold $200,000 worth of gold and silver in a single day.

That statement can be assumed to be true, indicative of considerable sales skills, and the unmistakable mark of someone who is *not* trying to avoid being rejected. If in fact this person were applying for a part-time job with a small precious metals dealer, the sentence might be okay, maybe. Otherwise the *part-time* may imply a lack of full commitment, *small* may, to a large firm, hint at a lack of adequate experience, and the *once* may suggest, to a cynical observer, a one-time result that was never repeated.

Your Choice of Words

A better choice of words for the individual who sold gold and silver would be to say "Personally sold as much as $200,000 of gold and silver in a single day." That's fine, but only if you are applying for a job selling precious metals. Should you want to use that experience to get a job in similar areas, you could instead say "Personally sold as much as $200,000 worth of valuable commodities in a single day."

Either way, your statement is still true and still indicative of considerable sales skills, but without the potential negatives in the original version.

You may want to use experience in one business to apply to a job in another. Rather than saying that you worked for a manufacturer, you may wish to substitute the word *company* or *firm* or *organization*. Using *company* for instance, does not necessarily create a similarity, but as long as you are not applying to an institutional or government employer, it cannot create a dissimilarity, which is a very important consideration if you do not know the exact nature of an employer's business.

How about the following: "A volunteer for the State Environmental Control Authority, I was active in monitoring air, water, and noise pollution."

The statement is fine with one exception: the word *volunteer*. People who are willing to pay a salary for work tend to have negative preconceptions about volunteer work as requiring less commitment and being much less demanding. They may be all wet, but why argue the point? Stay with what you have done rather than bring up aspects of your experience that won't help you. "Monitored air, water, and noise pollution for the State Environmental Control Authority" is factual; shows knowledge, skill, and experience; and has no negatives. It is conceivable that someone in private industry might prefer to hire pollution experts with industry experience, so why chance it? Rewrite the sentence and say: "Fully experienced in all phases of monitoring water, air, and noise pollution." No negatives there. Another possibility, also without negatives, is to say: "Monitored air, water, and noise pollution for a leading environmental testing organization."

Do not assume that employers will value people who are *adaptable* or *flexible*. Unless you are applying for a job as a lump of modeling clay, those characteristics are meaningless. To say that you are "experienced in dealing with a rapidly changing work environment" is fine, but *adaptable* sounds like you have no mind of your own. Remember to be guided by whether an employer specifically asked for that type of experience; if not, why are you bringing it up?

Implications

When you make it obvious that you are seeking your fourth job in three years, what do you expect employers to infer? That you have been investigating various career change options? That you were fired by your last three employers? That you are sick and tired of working for cheapskates who won't pay decent wages?

Those may be true and valid reasons for changing jobs as well as careers, but *from an employer's point of view*, those reasons may imply that you are unreliable, unsure of what you want to do, prone to whimsical job changes, short on loyalty, and long on greed. Unfortunately for you, your reasons for looking for work—when compared to the perceptions of most employers—are associated with employee qualities that bosses want very much to avoid.

A job-seeker with questionable reliability presents little hope to the employer and will also trigger his fears that problems might occur if the wrong person were hired. Who's going to want to experiment with someone whose application spells *p-r-o-b-l-e-m-s*? No one.

You can also get into trouble by implying that you are a take-charge individual. That's fine when you are certain that is what the employer wants, but otherwise, watch it! No employer wants to hire a bull in a china shop.

Emotions

Do not rock the boat! Here again, implying that you don't meet criteria or triggering adverse reactions to your personality can evoke annoyance, anger, fear, or intuitions that will combine to force the employer to view your application with trepidation.

Emotions can kill your job chances, and yet they are easy to avoid. *After* you have made a good impression and *after* the employer makes a pitch to get you, then emotions may become your ally should the employer fear that you'll go elsewhere.

Money

One last example of negatives to avoid is mention of your current salary. If that salary is higher than the employer wants to pay, you won't receive more consideration. Should you avoid this hangup and get an interview, however, you just might be able to convince the employer that you are good enough to justify his bending a bit on his budget. Who knows? The opportunities might be good enough for you to bend a bit on your salary demands; you'll never know if you squelch your chances by divulging salary.

Another reason for not giving your salary is that the company to which you are applying may, for any number of reasons, be willing to pay quite a bit more than you are now making. The trouble is that they won't do it if they know you are looking to them for a big increase in pay. Typical employer thinking indicates that you are paid what you are worth, and if you were worth a certain pay someplace else, that's what they believe you are worth to them.

Other applicants have done themselves out of a job or out of a nice increase by putting their current salary in their applications. Don't let that happen to you.

FALLING SHORT

What do you do if you come across a job specification in which you fall short in one or more areas? Perhaps the employer

- wants ten years experience and you have only five, or maybe even only two years under your belt.
- has asked for college degrees you don't have.
- requires experience in a business you've never worked in, although you have been in a related field.
- prefers someone who has been with a much larger or much smaller organization than your current or past employers.
- demands applicants who have worked in the private sector, whereas your experience has been in government work.

What you can do in these situations is to think for a few minutes and try to put your needs, values, and emotions aside so that your intelligence can control your decisions. If you are way out in left field in terms of what you can legitimately say compared to what the employer wants, you may be wasting your time by even trying for the job. If, on the other hand, you are convinced that you are on the threshold of a realistic stairway, that it represents a job-search journey that makes sense for you, and that you can handle the job, go ahead and apply. If you are kidding yourself, you will be wasting no one's time but your own.

There are three steps you can take when applying for jobs in which you think you may fall short of an employer's qualifications:

1. Don't mention the shortcoming. Don't point it out, don't explain it, don't offer excuses or alibis.

2. Divert the employer's attention from the unmentioned shortcoming to the areas where you *do* meet the criteria. Make a very strong case for yourself in each of those areas.

3. Use implications to imply that you do not fall short. In addition to the material in this chapter and in Chapter 4, Chapter 11 will show you how to present yourself so that employers will infer that you have no apparent weaknesses.

You may not be able to change someone's perceptions about qualifications, but don't get yourself out of step. Getting people to conclude that you should be offered the job takes place near the end of the hiring process, but getting them to conclude that you should be interviewed is accomplished in only the third step.

Worry about matching the hiring criteria later. At the outset, you have only to worry about whetting the employer's appetite and creating the *perception* that you are a good prospect. If you don't succeed in doing that, you'll never have to worry about hiring criteria because you'll never get interviews.

Sidestepping

In the minds of employers, shortcomings that are not perceived about you do not exist. The three-step approach outlined earlier will allow you to literally sidestep shortcomings in many instances as long as you are careful not to create implications that are impossible either to believe or to explain.

You can control your implications by developing and using a workable plan for each application. Ask yourself what you want to imply, how you can justify that implication when asked about it in interviews, and how to make your point so that you do not inadvertently imply negatives.

Sidestep whenever you fall short or think you may fall short of an employer's criterion. Rather than concentrating on or even bringing up the shortcoming, redirect the employer's attention to needs you *can* meet and values against which you compare favorably. That way, your written application can concentrate on the strengths that make you look good. If those strengths are attractive enough, the employer may be willing or even anxious to forget about the shortcoming. Similarly, a conversation can be directed to your strengths rather than your weakness.

You won't always be able to sidestep shortcomings, but if you haven't tried it, you'll be surprised; you can do it more often than you might imagine.

Respect the Employer's Intelligence

Bosses aren't dummies. If they were, they probably wouldn't be bosses. No, they don't make all their decisions intelligently, but then no one does. They also have values, needs, and emotions as does everyone else.

You are making a big mistake if you think that you are going to use the material in this or any other book to con, hoodwink, or psych-out employers. That can be done, but if you're not an expert at that sort of thing already, it would take longer to learn the required techniques than it would to get a job.

Using an employer's values, needs, and emotions to your advantage simply puts you a leg up compared to other applicants, and lets you deal with the employer on an informed basis relative to recognizing and dealing with criteria. When you feel informed, you are more comfortable with whatever you are doing and more apt to do it right.

When you do it right, you *will* get a good job. At that point, some employer is going to feel that he's made a pretty intelligent decision by hiring you.

Who are you to argue?

NOBODY LOSES

You know what you can do, what you like to do, and what income you need. If you lose control of your impulses and settle for anything less, it is nobody's fault but your own.

Being in control is mandatory to avoid being suckered into taking a job because you are blinded by mere *perceptions* of opportunity carefully crafted by smooth-talking employers. Watch out for those employers who will make vague promises of promotion or other advantages you might enjoy if you accepted their offer. Ask them to put it in writing; they may object to providing you with such written guarantees, but they should at least be willing to commit to when you would be reviewed for promised increases or promotions. Their refusal to provide that minimal backup to their offer should be taken as a clue that you should start looking elsewhere.

You also have to know what you are worth. Too many employers will jump at the chance to hire you for far less than they should if they sense that you are ignorant of the going wage for the type of work you seek. With a little bit of research, you can get a good idea of the present salary range. Aside from asking friends about wage scales, trade associations, government reports, and newspaper or magazine articles can give you excellent insight into current salaries. The librarian at any major library can help.

Being in control means more than making sure that you don't come out on the losing end of a job negotiation; it also means that you have to make sure that the employer also doesn't become a loser.

Why should you worry about the employer's not being a loser? Do employers worry about you?

Believe it or not, the good ones *do* worry about you. Smart employers are aware that if you don't like a job, you will eventually leave and take another. It is in their best interests to hire only people who will like the work, the pay, the people, and the opportunity. That way, they have a better chance of holding on to the people they hire.

The same philosophy applies to you. You must make an employer feel that he is a winner—not a loser—by hiring you. Otherwise, you'll never be able to motivate him to extend that offer to you rather than to someone else.

"Nobody loses" means that both you and the employer are winners when you get hired. You get a challenging job you want at a salary you can live with; the employer gets—at a price he can afford—the services of someone who is ready, willing, and able to do the job in a first-class manner. There is a mutuality of need, a mutuality of interest, and an agreement that there is good compatibility among you and all concerned parties.

Lastly, don't make the mistake of assuming that "nobody loses" means "nobody compromises." To the contrary, everybody compromises at one time or another. As long as you get something of value in terms of tangible rewards, written promises, or opportunities that would be difficult to duplicate, it is not only proper, but downright intelligent to compromise.

B. THE TECHNIQUES

8. Point Yourself in the Right Direction

A help-wanted advertisement may give you some indication of what an employer wants in the way of a "perfect" job candidate, but you have to spend a great deal of time talking to many employers before you can get a good, in-depth appreciation for what they *really* want. Fortunately, there is a better way to get that information. If you study and understand the list that follows, you'll be better equipped to understand employer thinking on job-candidate qualifications.

WHAT EMPLOYERS WANT

Employers usually look for certain characteristics which they think will result in their getting the best possible person for the job. Obviously, not all employers think alike, and not all jobs are filled according to the same general criteria. More often than not, however, a job you are after will involve a good sampling of the following:

Experience in a Specific Business With a Specific Product or Service

To many employers, this is the single most important criterion. They feel that if you have experience in their business, and with their products and services, that you'll better understand their needs, and you'll be able to be fully productive immediately, with no break-in period. These employers feel that their business is unique and that it requires someone who has been in it before.

Is it? Who knows. You have to remember that an employer doesn't know you, but he does know the difficulties of his business. If he believes that prior experience in that business is all-important, you had better be prepared to demonstrate such experience if you want the job.

It would be ridiculous to suggest that prior industry experience applies to all jobs, but it does apply to many management-level positions, some jobs in engineering (particularly in computer and electronic equipment fields), and jobs in various aspects of sales, marketing, and advertising. Furthermore, the "prior industry experience" criterion even extends into areas which surprise many people. Machinist jobs in the aerospace industry, for instance, have been known to require people who are familiar with the exacting standards of that industry.

Experience and Expertise in a Specific Type of Work

You've got to be able to demonstrate that you're a proven performer: that you have not only done a certain kind of work, but that you've done it exceptionally well. Employers want results, and the more you can do to show them that you have been a consistent producer of outstanding results, the better you can imply that you are capable of continuing such results on that next job.

A Specific Educational Background

Although you got out of school twenty years ago, some employers will require that you have a certain degree. Some may even ask your grades. To these people, it may not matter what you've done since school or how good you are; if you don't have the degree, you're going to have to be quite clever in sidestepping that issue (see Chapters 11 and 13).

Experience for a Specific Length of Time

Even if you have the right type of experience, an employer may feel that you haven't had enough of it. The more responsible the job, the more experience will be required. Most management jobs, for instance, will require five to ten years' experience of a "similar" nature.

A Consistent Employment Record

For a variety of reasons, many people leave (or are fired from) their jobs and go on to something else. Unfortunately, someone who has never been out of work may tend to think that unemployed people are either lazy, incompetent, uncooperative, or dishonest. An employer with that attitude is suspicious of anyone who is unemployed or has gaps in his or her employment record.

In a similar vein, you may have two strikes against you if you have frequently changed jobs or the type of work you have done. If an employer thinks you have difficulty holding jobs or that you become dissatisfied too easily, your image may be tarnished.

A "Match" in Income

No employer will offer you one penny more than he or she thinks is the lowest salary you'd accept. As an indication of what you might accept, employers often assume that if they can make the job sound sufficiently attractive, you may take the job at the same salary you're getting now.

It is also often assumed that no matter how attractive the job, few people are going to accept an appreciable decrease in income. For this reason, people indicating a given salary are looked upon with suspicion when they apply for a job offering less money.

Another consideration is that employers usually have a budget in mind when hiring. This budget indicates the maximum salary they can afford to pay. With some rigidly structured companies, if you indicate that your current salary or your salary demands are close to the maximum figure in their budget, you may be ruled out of the competition as soon as the employer sees your application. This is because the employer would feel that you would have no room to grow within their salary structure. A current salary above the employer's budget may also find your application quickly reaching the circular file.

Why contact an employer in a way which may automatically hurt your chances? Of course salary is important to you and will be a consideration in whether you accept a job. It is to your advantage, however, to sell yourself on performance and results *before* discussing salary.

Never mention or divulge salary information in a job application. In interviews, talk about salary only when the employer brings up the subject. (Salary discussions are covered further in Chapters 13 and 14.)

A "Match" in Career Progression and Goals

Indicating that you have been Vice-President of Sales may cause some employers to think that you might not be interested in a job which has the less lofty title of Sales Manager. As was previously mentioned, for all they know the vice-president of one company has less latitude and a lower income than the sales manager of their own company; there's no way that this can be proved or disproved, and unfounded doubts can too easily enter the picture.

Even beyond job titles, employers like people who have a potential for growing within the company, either in terms of handling progressively increasing responsibility on the same job, or of being promotable. If there is any indication that you might find a job to be boring or a step backwards in your career, you will quickly lose favor.

Someone considering you will not want to have to go through the hiring process all over again in order to replace you in the near future. Should you want to leave within a year in order to go into business for yourself, it's advisable not to so inform prospective employers.

The "Right" Personality

You need the right personality to succeed at a job, and you also need the right personality to get along with your boss. Before applying for a job, there's not much you can do about showing that you've got the right personality to get along with the person who will be your boss. Your best bet in this regard is to avoid extremes when applying. You can be confident of your abilities without being cocky, and you can be intelligent without being condescending.

As far as the job is concerned, showing that you have the right personality usually requires little more than common sense. A person with the perfect personality for a Marine Drill Sergeant, for instance, might have difficulty adjusting to life as a Librarian. Similarly, management people are supposed to have a take-charge approach to their work, while clerical people are supposed to take orders with ease. As a Researcher, you would be expected to be analytical, whereas you'd have to be tough and relentless as a Construction Foreman. Common sense.

A Good "Fit"

Every company has its own personality, made up of such factors as the politics of the organization, the people through whom certain activities must flow, the way the company reacts to different inside and outside pressures, and so forth.

In addition to rating you on your own attributes, an employer may therefore also rate you on the basis of how you would fit in with the existing scheme of things. You may be an individualist, a decisive doer. That's fine, except when applying to firms which operate on the team basis, with most decisions being made by committee.

When you're applying for a job, how can you tell whether you'd fit in from the employer's point of view? How can you tell whether you'd fit in from *your* point of view?

You can't. All you can do is to defer those questions to the time of the interview. If you're lucky, a bad fit will become apparent then, rather than after you have started on the job.

As you apply for jobs, personality factors and "fit" factors should be kept in the background until you have been able to sell yourself on the basis of performance and results. If you play up what you have done, while toning down individualistic aspects of your personality, you will be able to go after jobs in a manner which forces the employer to be objective, rather than subjective. If the objective aspects—performance, results, accomplishments—of your application do a good selling job for you and you have the employer interested, *then* you can discreetly use the interview process to find out more about the matter of "fit."

All of the Above—with References

That's right—an employer will want the sun, the moon, and the stars. The higher your responsibility, the higher your salary, the more exacting will be the demands of prospective employers.

Since they may have difficulty confirming what you say without outside corroboration, employers will ask you for references: names of people who can attest to the fact that you are a fine person and a dedicated worker.

Imagine the silliness of references. An employer doesn't know you, so he asks you to give him the names of references. He doesn't know any of the people on your reference list, either, but if they have corporate titles after their names, their word will be believed as gospel. For all the prospective employer knows, every one of your references is a close friend or relative of yours, but each will be called and dutifully asked to answer several questions.

In order to get around the fact that smart job-seekers will never give the names of people who will give anything less than perfect references, some employers ask for the names of the people to whom you reported on previous jobs so that those people can be contacted as references. *No* name should ever be divulged unless you are absolutely certain that, if contacted, the person will give you a perfect reference: not one that's so glowing as to sound phony, but one that expresses complete satisfaction in you and your work.

GOT A MATCH?

Even if you don't smoke, you are going to have to find a match if you want to get the right job! The kind of match you need for a job doesn't create flames, it creates offers. This kind of match is the common ground between what an employer thinks you have to offer and what that same employer thinks is needed to fill the job.

Fortunately, you do not have to be a mind reader to understand what an employer wants. All of the criteria listed above may be important to some employers, but the qualifications most typically given top priority relate to certain types of prior experience. Specifically, you'll do yourself a lot of good whenever you can show that you have been:

- in a business the same as or very similar to the employer's business.
- handling products and/or services very similar to those handled by the prospective employer.
- in a job very similar to the job at hand.

How about you? What have you done? For what kinds of companies? Take stock of your work experiences. What industries have you been in and with what products or services have you worked? Make a list and be specific; if you've been in the shoe business, was it with a manufacturer? a wholesaler? a retailer? Put it on the list.

What Are Your Skills?

For each job you've had, break down the work into its functional responsibilities and forget about job titles. As an example, if you've been a cab driver, you did not simply drive a taxi; you handled money, established routings, and were responsible for a vehicle. Similarly, if you were a sales manager, you may have been responsible for personnel management, plans and programs, sales, advertising, market research, and so on.

After you have made your list, go back to each activity at each job and see if you can *quantify* your output. If you were a typist, how fast are you in words per minute? If you were in sales, how much did you sell? If your job was in areas not measured by output, it can probably be measured by size: the size of the company, the number of students and classes you taught, the number of cases you handled.

The purpose of this list is not to help you decide what to do, but rather to let you know what kinds of employers might be interested in you for which kinds of jobs. In your particular case, that interest could be expressed in any of the areas on your list . . . IF the employer knew you were available and had a pertinent background.

Know What You Want

You cannot conduct any kind of rational job campaign without knowing specifically what you want to do, what type of future you expect from a job, where you would work, whether you would relocate, what level of income you need, and so forth.

What you want out of a job and out of life is not going to influence an employer to give it to you, but knowing your goals will enable you to aim your sights on those employers who come as close as possible to meeting your needs.

As an example, suppose your family circumstances make it impossible for you to relocate. This happens to many people; children are in school, their spouse works near home, and life would be completely disrupted by a move. If you found a very good job eighty miles from home, you'd have to decide whether the time and cost of commuting were worth the trouble. This is a priority decision that only you can make.

The same applies to various aspects of the job itself. Do you prefer a large or small organization? Are you unhappy unless you have a great deal of latitude in how you do your work? Can you function in a high-pressure environment? Do you want an employment contract? Are you more concerned with security of employment or high earnings potential? Can you get along with dictatorial bosses?

In terms of your income needs, don't look at total salary alone; think in terms of spendable income. Comparing where you are now with a new job means that you have to look at differences in commuting costs, company-paid insurance, taxes and methods of withholding tax deductions, and—if appropriate to your work—factors such as expense reimbursement and company cars. Also, you have to think not only about what you can make now, but also about your income potential and needs five or ten years from now. What are your current and future income objectives? Will the jobs you seek meet those objectives?

Most important is that you enjoy or at least can live with the type of work you do. Other than jobs you take temporarily to look into a given field or other potentially short-term situations you may accept until you find something better, there is no point in spending your life at work you don't like. Wouldn't you rather enjoy your work than hate it?

If You Are Switching Careers

Taking up another profession is not particularly easy, but it *can* be done as long as you are able to think about your work experiences in purely functional terms that can be applied elsewhere. A good example is a person who decides to switch from being an elementary school teacher to some other field.

Most of us think of teaching schoolchildren as educating and disciplining young people, but those activities are only a part of what a teacher does. Teachers also speak before a group, they are experienced in visual-aids presentations, they know how to plan their activities, they surely have worked in community relations, they can write, and they obviously have a background in setting up and implementing training programs. There aren't too many nonteaching jobs that can make use of skill in educating children, but these other activities can be applied in a multitude of businesses and institutions. Add in a knowledge of educational publications, and the list of possibilities gets even longer.

If you want to switch, don't tell prospective employers about your plans; don't even say anything about what you have done versus what you want to do. Make up your own list of functional experiences, and be prepared to apply them with a strong story about your skills and capabilities.

9.

Help-Wanted Ads and Other Job Leads

Contrary to what employment agencies or other job books tell you, help-wanted ads are one of the best sources of jobs. When a job is advertised, usually there *is* an opening. Depending on what the ad says, you may also know something about the employer's hiring criteria. In addition, you may also know what firm placed the ad and where they are located. You have the opportunity now to research them and their reputation with employees.

The only exceptions to this situation are ads placed by employment agencies or management recruiters and blind ads. A "blind" ad is one which asks you to respond to a box number, often in care of the publication in which the ad was placed. Employers use blind ads when they don't want applicants coming in unannounced or jamming their switchboards with phone inquiries. This kind of ad also prevents you from calling to find out what they thought of your application.

To identify those ads that are best for you, refer to both the criteria listed in Chapter 8 and to the work experience lists from that chapter. Concentrate on type of business, product or service, and functional responsibilities. Compare what is on your lists with each ad.

Do you have a match? Several possible matches? Respond to any advertised job you think you can handle, but don't forget that you'll be wasting your time and effort unless you can make the employer believe that you are qualified.

Where to Find Ads

Help-wanted ads are found in the daily classified sections of newspapers and also in different technical and trade journals. If you are looking for a job in a specific field, there may be a magazine or trade journal which also runs help-wanted ads. (You should find out—if you don't already know—whether your field is covered by such magazines.)

For jobs in management, engineering, accounting, law, and other so-called professional jobs, the business sections of many newspapers contain a number of ads. Although most newspapers are local in nature with respect to help-wanted ads, several papers feature ads from all over the country for these special job listings. The Sunday *New York Times*, for instance, has a large listing of executive and other highly skilled job ads in its financial section. It also has, in its Week in Review section, ads in the health (nursing, hospital administration, etc.), education (teaching, school management, etc.), and library science fields. Similar listings appear in many other Sunday newspapers or daily (the best days are Tuesday and Wednesday) in *The Wall Street Journal*.

Your local library is a good place to start searching for ads. Not only would the library have an assortment of newspapers, but also a number of the trade journals you might need to make your search complete. If you find the nearest library branch inadequate, go to the main branch or to a nearby college library. It'll be worth the trip.

What to Look For

Certain ads will have more potential for you than others. In order to identify those that have the most potential, first determine which ads look like they represent jobs you'd want if they were offered. Then look over each ad for what it says and analyze the ad in the following ways:

1. If the ad lists the functional responsibilities of the job, the employer may be willing to accept expertise in those functional responsibilities in lieu of experience in his business. This is a good lead to follow even if you haven't been in that business.

2. Should the ad indicate that applicants must have experience in a specific business, you may be wasting your time by applying unless you can make a case for having experience in that business. Many of these ads have what could be called up-front qualifications. They may ask for a specific academic degree, a certain number of years experience in the business, and even a requirement that you have worked at a certain level on the corporate ladder.

3. When an ad is vague, perhaps specifying only the title of the job, Chapters 7 and 8 will help you to make reasonably valid assessments of what the employer wants.

You may, of course, have experience of a nature closely related to that specified in an ad; you must learn to recognize appropriate similarities. As an example, salespeople handling a specific product line may be servicing customers who would be of interest to an employer handling an entirely different product.

Other similarities may exist relative to the type or size of business and your own experience. Certain fields—such as corporate law, accounting, or advertising—often require experience more related to a class of business rather than to a particular, specific product. If you were doing advertising for a toothpaste firm, you would probably be well received at a shampoo manufacturer but not a computer firm. In a similar vein, if you were in the legal department of a $20 million company, you would probably have a hard time getting a job as Chief Corporate Counsel for a billion-dollar conglomerate.

Since each job-seeker's needs, experiences, and capabilities are different, it is virtually impossible to provide a "cookbook" list of similarities you should seek. You have to study the ads carefully and in depth, asking yourself the basic question: Can I convince this employer that I am a match with his needs? If you are not certain whether a specific ad represents potential for you, pursue it anyway. What do you have to lose?

RESPONDING TO THE ADS

Once you've located the ads that seem worth following up, there are a variety of ways to make that initial contact with the employer. Depending on the advertisement, you may have a choice as to how to respond.

Situations in Which You Should Apply in Person

When responding to a help-wanted ad that indicates applicants should apply in person, do so without wasting time. For these jobs, people are often hired on the spot; so get there early, be first in line, and give it your best effort. If you show up after someone else is hired, you lose!

Theoretically, you can apply in person to any employer whose identity you know. The direct approach provides you with a way to skip the intermediate steps in the employment process, allowing you to make a fast and powerful first impression—*if* you can get an interview. Chapter 13 will show you how to control interviews.

You must, however, reach the person making the hiring decision. The problem is that unless they invite applicants to come in without a prior appointment, employers may be out, busy, or otherwise unwilling to meet with you unless you first call or write.

Situations in Which You Should First Use Your Telephone

As with in-person applications, telephone applications put you in the position of having to motivate someone to want to take the time to interrupt his or her schedule to listen to your sales pitch. If the employer isn't hiring in your field, the best you'll get is a perfunctory suggestion that you send in a résumé.

When, on the other hand, a help-wanted ad states the name and address of the employer without saying that applicants should apply in writing, you have nothing to lose by calling and asking for an appointment.

Getting to the right person is critical. You should speak directly with the person to whom you would report if you get the job. If you don't know the name of that person, call and ask. Identify the ad if you are calling in response to an advertised job. If the opening was not advertised, and you are trying to find out whether one exists, ask for the name of the person who has the title of the person to whom you'd most likely report.

If all you can get is the personnel department, you will probably be asked to send in a résumé. The only exceptions will occur when you luck out and call at precisely the same time that the employer is looking for someone with just your skills. Don't be discouraged if you are told that there is an opening and they prefer people to apply in writing. Fine. Apply in writing, but while you have them on the phone, get some information: to whom does the job report, what level of experience do they want, are any particular skills emphasized in the job description, and is it a new job or would you be replacing someone?

Then, when you write in, you have information on which to base your sales pitch. Also, you know the name of the person who is probably your key to getting the job: your prospective boss. Be sure to send him a copy of anything you send in.

Techniques for handling telephone conversations are described along with interviewing techniques in Chapter 13, because a telephone application can become a telephone interview in the blink of an eyelash. Other than the opening sentence or two, they are the same and are best treated as such.

Situations in Which You Should Apply in Writing

Virtually any responsible job that can have serious operational or financial effects on a company will require a written submittal. Any help-wanted ad with a blind box-number response also requires a written application.

For out-of-town jobs, you are going to have to submit a written application if you expect the employer to reimburse for your travel expenses. It is unrealistic for either you or the employer to spend that money unless there is some evidence that you are a good match with their needs. Were you to have to bear the expense of interview trips without reimbursement, you would quickly be out of funds, unless you knew in advance that there was a good chance of success.

Why should an employer take the time to talk with you on the telephone, much less in person? Particularly when you are applying for a responsible job with a good salary, catching the employer when he or she is unprepared for your sales pitch will generally provide you with less than satisfactory results. Not only will employers balk at traveling to interviews or paying your travel expenses without justification, they will also object to taking the time to talk about a responsible job with someone about whom they know nothing.

These situations are best handled by written applications.

THE BENEFITS OF WRITTEN APPLICATIONS

When you apply for a job, you often know a great deal about the employer. You usually know the business the employer is in, the type of work you would do if you were hired, and—if you are responding to a help-wanted ad—the qualifications established for getting the job.

But what does that employer know about you? Only what you want him to know; no more and no less. Since written communications cannot result in instantaneous replies, you can compose outstanding applications over a period of hours, and you have the luxury of being able to plan answers to any questions the employer may ask later on. That way, *you* have control.

Another reason for writing is that a written application can be read and reviewed at the employer's convenience. You therefore do not have to force your message on anyone's busy schedule. If you do a good enough job of whetting the reader's appetite, you'll get a response—assuming, of course, that the employer has a need for the services you offer.

Written communications therefore give you the chance to plan and orchestrate your attack and to tailor each application to the particular employer to whom it is being sent.

WHY NOT USE RÉSUMÉS?

There are three reasons for not using résumés:

1. As discussed on page 3, a résumé is a "list of the ingredients" in your career. Rather than telling a prospective employer of the benefits to be derived from hiring you, a résumé provides numerous facts and details from which the reader must draw his or her own conclusions. With only these facts and details, it is simply too difficult for you to be certain that those conclusions will be to your advantage. A far better approach is to send

a well-written letter that implies those conclusions you want drawn and compels the reader to contact you for the facts and details necessary to support those conclusions. Your message to an employer, whether in person, over the telephone, or in writing, must be that hiring you will benefit that employer. That message must be direct and the benefits you offer must be clearly indicated in terms of the productivity, effectiveness, efficiency, or profitability of the organization. The employer should not have to figure out or decipher those benefits from an array of the ingredients of your career.

2. A job application must be carefully aimed at giving you an image which is totally positive. Each application must be tailored to indicate that you are the perfect candidate for the job at hand. You have to be selective about the information provided in applications. Which information will help your cause with which employer? Which information will hurt you? No one résumé, no matter how well it is written, can possibly do you justice at any variety of prospective employers. With résumés, your work experience is a completely open book. Rather than providing a prospective employer with a hard-hitting letter which concentrates on only those factors which are most likely to impress that particular employer, a résumé will bury the reader with all kinds of information. Some of that information will help you, some will hurt and you cannot adequately tailor your approach.

3. Résumés are frequently the wrong length. If you've had a number of jobs over a period of years, your résumé may be several pages long. Sorry, but it is virtually impossible to get your point across if it takes two, three, or four pages. It is also unrealistic to expect anyone to read, digest, and properly (from your point of view) interpret such a long document when it is submitted as a job application.

Look at the experts in selling: the people who sell soap, automobiles, toothpaste, cosmetics, and even our old friend, shampoo. Do these people bury you with technical details? Do they leave it up to you to figure out what a product will do for you?

No. They sell benefits. With all the subtlety of a runaway freight train, they tell you what their product will do for you, the manner in which it will improve your life, or the degree to which it will make you a happier person.

This does not mean that you can sell your services in the same tone as a toothpaste commercial, but it does mean that you *must* sell your services on the basis of convincing the prospective employer that hiring you would be beneficial to the organization—more beneficial than would be the case were anyone else hired.

Résumés are an ineffective way to sell benefits. With the right job-application letters, you can accept the fact that employers demand perfection in job candidates, and use that fact to your own advantage by introducing them to that perfect candidate: you!

WRITING APPLICATIONS

When you respond in writing to a help-wanted ad, proceed as follows:

1. Write a neat, error-free, typewritten letter that is completely contained on one side of one sheet of standard-size white stationery (more about writing such letters in Chapter 10).

2. Tell the employer how you meet every qualification listed in the ad. Sidestep or circumvent (see Chapters 11 and 13) criteria you don't meet.

3. If the ad mentions a business, product, or service, show whatever similarities you can. If the ad is vague but mentions the employer's name, go to a library or use your telephone to identify the employer's business. Again, show similarities if you can. Otherwise, don't say what business you've been in.

4. Give examples that show how good you are at the type of work for which you are applying.

5. Compose and type a separate letter in response to each ad. You cannot possibly address yourself to answering the specifics of each ad unless you use separate letters every time. You may choose to use letters which are similar and which use identical sentences or even identical paragraphs, but unless your letters are individually composed, you will not be able to tailor each letter to the ad to which it is a response.

TARGETED EMPLOYERS

Some employers may be advertising to fill openings, and you will come across their ads. In other cases, however, you may not have read the publication in which their ads appeared, they may not yet have advertised, or they may have run their ads before you started looking but may still be interested in talking to people. They may also be working through an employment agency or management recruiter.

Accordingly, you should plan and begin a job campaign to make known your availability and qualifications to all potential employers in the area you wish to work. This means that you have to decide the distance you would want to commute and whether you could and would relocate to a given area in order to take the right job.

Next, you have to identify those employers who would be most likely, within the geographical area of interest to you, to hire you if they had an opening. This is accomplished by use of directories to determine which employers could be a match, followed by an extensive campaign to advertise yourself to each such employer. It stands to reason that employers with job openings can be persuaded to hire you if you have had relevant experience. It also stands to reason that the burden is on *you* to make them aware of your availability and of the considerable benefits you offer.

Directories

One of the first directories to look in is the yellow pages of telephone books in localities of interest to you. Retail businesses, wholesalers, travel agencies, realtors, manufacturer's representatives, schools, hospitals, law firms, printers, advertising agencies, and many different types of manufacturers, suppliers, and service businesses advertise in the yellow pages.

In addition, for every state there is an industrial directory which lists manufacturers of various products, material suppliers, industrial distributors, contractors, and service businesses ranging from printers to artists to security firms to computer programmers. These directories are classified by type of business—manufacturer, distributor, wholesaler, or service business—and also by product or service. The name and address of each firm is listed, often along with the names of the people who run the company.

In case industrial or telephone directories aren't right for your needs, you should find out whether there is a directory for the specific type of business you are targeting. Some trade publications, for instance, publish directory issues which list names and addresses of businesses in a particular field. You can obtain directories geared to companies in many different businesses, including computers, electronics, pharmaceuticals, chain stores, and others.

Still another type of directory contains names and addresses of major corporations classified by type of business. If corporate headquarters are your targets, Standard & Poor's *Register of Corporations, Directors, and Executives,* and the Dun & Bradstreet *Million Dollar Directory* will be of interest to you. Each of these directories is national in scope, but may be of limited value if you target a branch location of a listed company. As an example, many of the major pharmaceutical companies in the United States have headquarters in and near New York City. If someone wanted to work in production management for one of these companies, he or she might be better off applying to the manufacturing locations rather than the main offices. These people have to use trade directories or state industrial directories.

Trade associations also have their own directories, but these are in some cases available only to members. It never hurts, however, to ask if there is an association of manufacturers in a market you are pursuing. Check it out. Trade journals can also be an excellent reference source. If a journal doesn't give a trade association reference, call or write the editor and you'll probably get a lead on where you can get a good list of prospective employers.

Other Resources

A *good* library is obviously a necessity for the references listed above. While you're there, you should look at a book called *Business Publication Rates and Data.* This is a large volume published monthly for the advertising industry as a reference of advertising rates and publication circulation figures. This reference is also very helpful to the job-seeker, since it contains trade journals classified by type of business. It will probably give you a lead on which if any of those journals would help you. Addresses and telephone numbers are given with each listing, making it easy for you to follow up such leads.

Two other sources for names of employers are available from the better libraries. One is a telephone reference service which will enable you to call in and ask questions such as whether there is a trade association in a particular business and, if so, where it is located. The second is a book entitled *The Directory of Directories.* This book will involve a good deal of research, but if you can't find other sources, use it to identify other directories which will help you.

PURSUING TARGETED EMPLOYERS
Making Phone Calls

To pursue these targeted job possibilities, you have to list a number of employers and call each to ask whether they have any openings. If you prefer, you can say that you heard that they had openings and you are calling for information and details. What's the worst they can say to you?

Even if they are advertised, however, management, engineering, marketing, accounting, and other so-called professional jobs are another story. The criteria for these jobs are highly specific, and the jobs may involve a great deal of responsibility. There is too much at stake in these situations for employers to decide anything over the telephone. You may be able to get information about the job, and you may be able to get an interview, so you should always try, but don't be surprised if you don't always succeed.

What did you expect? A bed of roses and a marching band to greet you whenever you apply? Even if you can use the telephone only to identify prospects, do it! Yes, telephoning has its drawbacks. Secretaries screen calls, people are always in meetings, and it isn't easy to simultaneously find out what the employer wants and point out how you're it. That's why you need strength in numbers. You are being unrealistic if you start out with a telephone list of ten targeted employers; you should never have less than at least fifty at a time.

What's that? You say there's not more than fifty employers where you live? Could be, but are you chained to the ground? Can you not look elsewhere? If not, you have other priorities that obviously conflict with your ability to find work. You'd better decide which is more important.

Written Applications to Targeted Employers

When you write to targeted employers, start with a list of at least a hundred. If those do not produce results, pick another hundred, and another, until you get a match. This means that you had better be a productive and accurate typist, or at least have access to such a typist. Otherwise, you'll have to "hunt and peck" at your typewriter and spend a great deal of time producing letters.

There is, however, a better way to get the same results. As stated in Chapter 8, you have to pick employer targets on the basis of which employers would be most likely to hire you IF they had an opening, IF they knew of your availability and expertise, and IF you do a good job of convincing them that *you* were the person they should hire. Once you have picked a list of targets, you should separate that list into categories.

These categories are based on a determination of which targeted employers could get the same letter. As an example, suppose that your field is Hospital Public Relations. It would therefore be reasonable for you to contact all hospitals in the geographical area of interest to you. You might also, however, want to contact public relations firms, advertising agencies, and institutions, such as colleges, civic organizations, foundations, and political organizations that utilize the same kind of public relations programs as do hospitals.

You therefore have a total of seven categories on your target list. To the hospitals on your list, you would write a letter that would highlight your experience and accomplishments in that field. To the other targets, you would write a different letter to each category, mentioning your experience and accomplishments in the field of public relations for "institutional organizations serving the general public."

This technique applies to many fields other than Hospital Public Relations. Assume, for instance, that a controller for a manufacturing company seeks employment elsewhere. The top financial executive for a $20 million company, however, will probably not be considered as a candidate for the job as top financial executive at a $5 billion company although the larger firm may very well have responsible, well-paid jobs that our controller friend could fill. Accordingly, this controller might write one letter to firms of approximately the same size as his current employer, and another letter to firms of much larger size.

The first letter could seek controller-type jobs and reference his current level of responsibility in terms of company size, whereas the second letter would seek "responsible financial management at corporate or division level" and reference his current level of responsibility in terms of having "financial management responsibility in a corporate environment." Both letters would heavily stress accomplishments.

In addition to the above two letters, the controller might also further categorize into businesses similar to that of his current employer and businesses which are different but similar in terms of their financial management needs.

Once you have separated your targets into categories, each target in each category can receive the same basic letter. Instead of writing a different letter for each target, you have to write a separate letter only for each basic category. Having composed such letters, you can then exercise some options which let you print form letters that don't look like form letters.

Each letter to a targeted employer should:

- Be addressed to the individual to whom you would report if you were hired. Preferably, this should be done in terms of the name of the individual and his or her job title. If you cannot get the name, call the employer and ask the operator for the name of the person who has the job title of the person to whom you would probably report. If such calling is prohibitively expensive, address your letters to that job title.

- If you've properly categorized your targets, each of your letters will be written so as to be addressed specifically to the needs and wants inherent in each category. Each recipient should feel that your letter was written for his or her eyes only. This can be done by showing similarities so that people perceive you to be ideal to suit their needs.

- The letter should be neatly typewritten on one side of one sheet of white, standard-size stationery. *No résumés.*

INTRODUCTIONS

Resources often overlooked in job-getting are friends, industry contacts, accountants, lawyers, and others who you know. Not that people in any of these categories would have a job to offer, but they might know someone who does, or they might know someone who knows someone else. To use these resources, you are not requesting charity and you certainly are not admitting incompetence, but you *are* being smart; you never know when someone might hear of an opportunity and pass it on to you. Even better, you might get the benefit of a direct introduction to an employer who *is* hiring. That way, you can zip right in and get an interview without having to go through the hassle of sending in an application.

Don't expect others to solve your personal employment problems, but don't pass anything up either. Just keep in mind that your friends know you as friends; they are in no position to sell you as a potential employee. The same goes for industry contacts; you have to sell yourself.

You should also expect some introductions to be mere favors granted by people who can't help you at all. If your time is limited, you may care to screen introductions by telephone to make sure that they will not waste your time.

ADVERTISING IN THE SITUATIONS-WANTED SECTIONS OF NEWSPAPERS AND MAGAZINES

Household help, baby-sitters, and people who provide services from their homes (typing services, fix-it services, etc.) may be able to effectively use this means of advertising their availability. Those who might use these services constitute a very wide cross section of the population, and targeting potential users is impractical, if not impossible, any other way.

In virtually all other situations, however, chances are that this kind of ad will result in your getting responses from numerous employment agencies and no one else. Do you really think that employers look for top people in the situations-wanted sections of magazines and newspapers? Be assured that those who do constitute a very tiny percentage of the employers who need good people.

It is tough enough describing yourself on a full page of type, much less in four or five lines of small-print classified advertising. How would you aim your message? To which potential employers? How could you, in such a small space, do a good job of spelling out the benefits you offer?

You can't do yourself justice with this kind of ad. Furthermore, for the cost of such an ad, you can write, type, and mail personalized, custom-tailored letters to hundreds of targeted employers. Which approach makes more sense to you?

EMPLOYMENT AGENCIES AND MANAGEMENT RECRUITERS

Employment agencies and management recruiters are service firms who, for a fee usually paid by client companies, help those companies fill job openings. Specifically, agencies and recruiters identify and screen candidates who meet qualifications provided by the employer. If you contact an agency, they'll ask you in for an interview if they're interested, but the first interview will be with them and not with the employer.

Even before that interview, you'll probably be asked to fill out an application form. Typically, such a form will ask for your background in terms of current and prior employer identification, job titles you've had, products with which you have worked, dates of employment, reasons for leaving, and so on. If you expect agency forms to leave space for you to indicate how well you did at a particular job or what accomplishments you have achieved, you will be disappointed.

An employment agency is in business to satisfy its clients' needs, not yours. It therefore strives to find job candidates who meet the job specifications set by its clients. The agency really doesn't care about your expertise if you do not perfectly fit those specifications. Even if you do fit the specifications, you have no chance of selling yourself to the employer; the agency does this for you. This puts you at a potential disadvantage, since the agency really doesn't care who gets the job as long as the employer is happy. No agency identifies just one potential employee for each job, so when your information is passed on to the employer, it will be accompanied by information on several others. In addition, agencies have their own ideas on how to impress clients, so whatever you send to the agency will probably be rewritten before the employer sees it.

This is one of the pitfalls of working through third parties to get a job. It's hard enough getting a job that meets all your needs without having to rely on someone who is not necessarily in your corner. Many people get jobs through agencies and recruiters. If that weren't the case, the agencies would quickly go out of business. If you seek a job in a clerical or secretarial function, or if you are in sales without any management experience or inclinations, you may find agencies to be quite helpful.

If, however, you are in management or a high technology field, agencies may be of less value to you. Salaries are higher, specifications become more and more detailed, and you lose too much control over how you are presented. You *may* be better than the person who gets the job, but unless the agency thinks you measure up, the employer will never be told that you exist.

Should you communicate with agencies and recruiters? Is it worthwhile to apply for jobs they are trying to fill for their clients?

Certainly; you have nothing to lose and you may find a good opportunity.

Can you assume that all agency fees are employer-paid? There's no need to assume anything. Ask.

Can you rely on agencies to get you a job? No. *You* are the only person on whom you can rely.

EMPLOYMENT COUNSELORS AND RÉSUMÉ WRITERS

Employment counselors come in various forms and provide various services. Some firms attempt to help people to better focus their career goals, to determine which employers would be prime prospects for jobs, and to chart a course of action.

In other cases, these firms will—for a fee that *you* pay—conduct a job-search campaign geared toward getting you a job. Very few, if any, of these outfits will give you any kind of guarantee that your money will get results; they get paid for trying, not succeeding.

Employment counselors—sometimes called outplacement counselors—can be expensive, so if you consider their use, check them out and make sure the costs are clearly spelled out in advance. After that, however, don't be surprised if the advice they give you is very similar to what you have already read in this book.

Résumé writers? Résumés? Ugh!

10. Letters That Work for You

The advertising and public relations industries have spent billions of dollars to research and develop effective ways of communicating with people in print. Since application letters are written communications, job-seekers would be better off if they used some of the techniques developed by the advertising experts. Chapter 11, Leading Inferences, goes into several of these techniques, but before that, you should think in terms of a basic approach used in designing advertisements. This approach might be called the ACBC of advertising:

A. Get the *Attention* of the reader.

C. Make a *Claim* about your product.

B. *Back* up that claim: justify it.

C. *Call* for action: ask the reader to take action if he or she is interested in your product.

This means that you have to get the employer's attention, claim that you would benefit the employer if you were hired, back up your claim with evidence showing how good you are, and ask the employer to take action in response to your letter.

Your letter can combine the first two points in a single paragraph merely by making a claim that gets the reader's attention. What kind of claims will get a reader's attention? Suppose you opened a letter with a question:

Could you use a first-rate purchasing agent?

With this question the applicant claims to be a first-rate purchasing agent and, in the same sentence, asks for a job. Unfortunately, however, this opening sentence gives the reader no reason for reading further. If the reader's gut reaction is to say no, the remainder of the letter may not be read. Even worse would be a sentence which read:

> I am looking for a job.

That opener is absolutely awful: it doesn't make the reader want to read more. By itself, your wanting a job is of no interest to a total stranger.

In your opening paragraph, you must make the reader care—to read further. This paragraph is your "grabber": it grabs and rivets the reader's attention to the rest of what you have to say:

> Having moved to Baltimore after eight years of successful linen sales experience in New York, it seems only natural that my background would enable me to benefit your operation in several ways.

Similarly, a sales manager candidate might open with:

> Following my promotion to sales manager for a firm similar to yours, I established and managed plans, programs, and personnel in two national sales organizations. After four years, the result of my efforts was a 225 percent sales increase accompanied by a 30 percent growth in profits. Now that I am looking for new horizons and challenges, accomplishments like the following can now be achieved on your behalf.

The only other thing you might want to do is to make it clear that you are now employed and in the same business, if true on both counts.

> Currently an Administrator for another Health Services Organization, I have established and managed plans, programs, and a staff of several dozen people. After three years, my efforts have resulted in a 60 percent increase in productivity with a 22 percent reduction in staff. Now that I am looking for new challenges, results like the following can be achieved on your behalf.

If you can't open with a flurry of statistics, you should at least be able to show familiarity with the type of work, type of business, or product.

> For the past five years, I have been the typesetter and paste-up artist for a small advertising agency. Having mastered the technical end of that business, I am now seeking opportunities to put the following creative accomplishments to better use.

When responding to a help-wanted ad, you usually do not have to identify the subject of your letter, but it doesn't hurt, particularly if you can do it without taking up excessive space.

> My experience is virtually identical to the qualifications stated in your advertisement. I have established and maintained an accounts payable and disbursements bookkeeping system for a company similar to yours, and recently combined the two on a "one-write" basis. Although still on that job, I am looking for new opportunities and the following achievements are directly applicable to your needs.

You can claim to be qualified when responding to an ad which lists qualifications for the job, but when writing to targeted employers, you don't know what they want, so your claim has to be implied by virtue of your expertise and familiarity with their type of business or product.

In each of the foregoing examples, note how the reader has to go no further than the opening paragraph to determine the purpose of the letter. First, however, the writer of each paragraph has been "positioned" as a person who is qualified, competent, and available. If an opening exists in the work area indicated, the reader will, in all probability, read the rest of those letters in detail.

Now you can go on to the B part of your letter. Here is the place to back up your claim: to show how good you are. This can be done by listing achievements which mean efficiency, productivity, effectiveness, or profitability to the prospective employer. A list of four or five achievements is a good indication of substantial expertise. If you can't come up with half a dozen like the following, you aren't trying hard enough:

> Successfully introduced five new products in three years.
>
> Implemented new security programs which cut energy costs by 34 percent.
>
> Taught eleven classes at three campuses while managing a $475,000 research grant and publishing three papers.
>
> Reorganized administrative staff and functions, resulting in a 22 percent reduction in personnel costs accompanied by 14 percent less overtime and a 47 percent increase in productivity.
>
> Conceived and organized six successful promotions in your field.
>
> Organized and managed the largest construction project in Europe.

Obviously, the same person would not have done all of the above, but the idea is the same in each case. They are hard-hitting accomplishments which will mean something to the reader—spaced so that each one stands out and nothing gets lost in a quicksand of paragraphs.

With some jobs, it is difficult or impossible to quantify accomplishments. In those situations, you might try the following approaches:

Complete familiarity with COBOL, A-FORTRAN, and X-BASIC languages.

One hundred ten error-free words per minute typing ability.

Completely fluent in French, German, and Arabic.

Experienced in all phases of tax-audit bookkeeping.

Handled all secretarial requirements for five executives.

In the last case, the writer could have said "people" rather than "executives." In applying for an executive secretary's job, however, the sentence carries more weight as shown.

The accomplishments in the B part of your letter need not all be from the same job or from the job referenced in your opening paragraph. You should merely list the achievements without comment as to when or on which job they occurred.

After the list of achievements, proceed to part C. This can be done with no more than two paragraphs, totaling eight lines including a double space between paragraphs, and can add information which is essential to your cause. Most importantly, it will make a call for action on the part of the reader or inform the reader of action you will take:

A BME graduate of Rutgers University, I have a record of ten years of continuous personal and professional growth. I would therefore be happy to meet with you to discuss my experience and to explore ways in which I might be an asset to your company.

To that end, I will call your secretary next week to determine when such a meeting would be most convenient for you.

or

After meeting or exceeding performance quotas for six consecutive years, my record in this field is second to none.

May I have an appointment to further discuss this matter with you at your convenience? I look forward to your early reply.

Notice how, without being arrogant or pushy, you make it clear that you mean business. The reader knows exactly what you want and what you are seeking as a result of your letter.

You should also take note of the fact that this letter format is quite flexible. When responding to help-wanted ads, for instance, you can also show correlation to the stated qualifications just about any place in the letter. If you feel more comfortable in using the B part for that purpose, fine. Otherwise, the previous examples show alternative methods which may be better adapted to your needs and writing style.

Should you prefer, you can use words, phrases, clauses, sentences, or even paragraphs from this book, as long as you intelligently substitute the particulars of your background for those of the fictitious people described above.

In case you're wondering, your spouse, your children, and the associations to which you belong have not been forgotten. These important parts of your life are indicative of your stability as a mature and responsible person, but it is highly unlikely that you will make a better first impression only because you are married and have a certain number of children. Unless that kind of information is necessary to show how you meet a known criterion, save it for the interview and use every bit of available space in your letter for addressing the employer's known or probable needs.

OTHER STYLES AND FORMATS

There are, of course, other formats which can be used in writing job applications. Your library should have several good books on composing business letters, and you may even have a style of your own with which you feel comfortable. Should you prefer something other than the format described above, however, you should ask yourself the following questions.

1. Does your letter grab the reader's attention? Does it hold it?

2. Does your letter enable the reader to see how good you are? Does it let the reader see your worth at a glance, without having to wade through wordy paragraphs?

3. Does your letter make it obvious that you would be a benefit to the employer? Are those benefits clearly stated or implied?

4. Does your letter show evidence to support your claims?
5. Does your letter call for action or tell what action you propose?
6. Does your letter meet the criteria for ad response or target employer letters (see pages 107–114)
7. Is your letter businesslike?

You be the judge.

TECHNICAL ASPECTS

Use 8½ by 11-inch white paper of a good quality, preferably with what is known as 25 percent rag content. White paper of this quality is professional and not garish. Although some people feel that colored paper will make their letters stand out from the pack, such paper simply does not look as good as white paper, and it is also more difficult to correct typing errors.

Any local printer can supply you with quantities of paper with your name, address, and telephone number typeset and printed across the top.

Efficient Usage of Space

Your letterhead can be designed to maximize the space for your sales pitch. This can be done by using type large enough to be easily read while occupying as little space as possible. You can then imprint the necessary information on no more than two lines, starting out about one inch down from the top of the sheet (see Figure 2).

Figure 2

R. A. JONES   123 MAIN STREET   ANYTOWN, ILLINOIS 09655
212-999-3838

or

ALAN W. STEWART   5 JOHNSON CIRCLE   SAN DIEGO, CA 10762
914-936-1616

Each letter should be dated three lines down from your letterhead imprint and starting twenty spaces to the left of your right-hand margin. Leave margins as narrow as possible, preferably ten spaces from both the left and right sides of the page. Start addressing the letter one line lower than date; two lines beneath the address information, type your salutation. After another two spaces, you can begin your first paragraph, the A and C parts of your letter. This arrangement uses the large open space in the upper right corner of the sheet without taking up a line you could otherwise use to sell your benefits to the prospective employer. A typical letter might therefore start as shown in Figure 3.

Figure 3

ALAN W. STEWART   456 SMITH STREET   ALBANY, NY 42606
202-755-8660

                                        May 16,1978

Box 4534 Times
The Cincinnati Times
434 Lakeshore Circle
Cincinnati, Ohio 16456

Gentlemen:

When in doubt, use "Gentlemen" as your salutation. It may not be accurate in some cases, but you'll be right most of the time.

Type your letter single spaced, but apply double spacing between paragraphs and also between accomplishments. After your second C ending, leave two or three spaces and sign off.

When you sign off, the safest bet is the traditional "Very truly yours." You should then sign your name boldly in black ink—like John Hancock did. Edit to put your signature at no less than about one inch above the page bottom. Since your name is typeset atop the page, there is no need to type it again beneath your signature.

Typewriter Equipment

If you do not have one, buy or rent an electric typewriter. The specifications of the correct typewriter are as follows:

- It should type twelve characters per inch of space. This spacing gives twenty percent more information per page than typewriters which give only ten letters per inch.
- Not all typewriters accept a carbon film ribbon, but yours should. An ordinary nylon ribbon gets used over and over, with the ribbon providing an increasingly lighter impression as it is used.
- With the carbon film ribbon, each impression is as sharp and as clear as the next. You get a clearer, sharper image.
- Your typewriter should have a good transparent paper guide so you can line up letters and lines so that you can individually address pre-printed letters.

Form Letters That Don't Look Like Form Letters

Suppose you are writing to several categories of targeted employers. Every letter in the same category can be identical to every other letter in that category except for the address and the name of the recipient.

You can, of course, type each individual letter separately, but this could be extremely time consuming if you have hundreds of letters in each category. Another approach would be to have your letters typed by a secretarial service. Type the letter yourself first, however, before having it done on the outside. This procedure will let you set the spacing and margins, thereby assuring that everything fits properly on the page.

There are also other ways to get large numbers of letters typed. Some service companies sell time on their word processing equipment. With this equipment, they will feed your letter into the machine and then feed in each name and address on your target list. Automatically, the machine then types out, on your paper, an individual letter to every one of your targets. Again, type it out yourself first to make sure of spacing and specify the type size and margins to be used.

Lastly, you might want to consider a do-it-yourself method that is almost as good as having individually typed letters, while costing less than the techniques described above.

Once you have an impressive letter, type it on a sheet of your letterhead but leave enough space to address the letter later. Do not type in the name and address of the recipient, the date, or the salutation. Merely leave enough space for all of this: sixteen spaces down from your typeset name and address. Use a carbon film ribbon. If you make errors, neatly correct them with fluid, tape, or correction ribbon.

Then have your letter printed in quantity by a local photo-offset. Do *not* have the letters printed on a photocopier; the photo-offset process gives *perfect* copies, including an almost perfect match with the darkness of the ink on your original.

You will now have a stack of your letterheads with what appears to be a typed letter on each sheet. To use these letters, you have to line-up the letters on your typewriter so that you can address, date, and add a salutation to each letter. After you individually sign each letter, the only way to tell that it has been printed is to turn it over and note the absence of impressions through the paper in the body of the letter.

You will, of course, have to experiment a bit to be able to perfectly line up the margins, but this can be done with the aid of the plastic guide on your typewriter. Using a film ribbon is critical here, since that is the only type of ribbon which has a consistent darkness. If your printer gives you a perfect ink match, this technique will work quite well. If he doesn't, it's because of sloppy work which you should refuse to accept.

It is up to you to ask the printer whether he will be able to get absolutely perfect copies of your letter. It is up to the printer, however, to tell you whether certain corrections or smudges will show up, and then to deliver the goods as promised.

SAMPLE LETTERS

The following pages contain an assortment of sample job application letters. Note how the strengths of each applicant can be seen in a matter of seconds.

All of these letters have been written according to the ACBC guidelines, but Letters 2 and 4 have the B part in paragraph form. Furthermore, Letters 6 and 7 are essentially the same, with the latter not identifying which achievement goes with which employer. Any of these formats will work, but if you have to highlight diverse accomplishments, the layout in Letters 1, 3, 5, or 7 may better allow each career milestone to stand out.

Should your experience be entirely in one industry and you are applying to an employer in the same industry for a similar job, choice of format would depend entirely on how many accomplishments you want to talk about and the complexity of each.

LETTER 1

For the past five years, I have been an Area Sales Manager for a company in your field. During that time, the results of my efforts were a 61 percent increase in the number of customers and a 250 percent growth in profitable sales. The following shows that my experience and capabilities are directly applicable to your needs:

- Identified and trained an average of 22 successful new distributors each year.

- Organized and conducted trade shows which brought in more than $2 million in sales.

- Personally sold orders as large as $300,000.

- On a first-name basis with all major customers in the tri-state area.

- Completely familiar with all phases of investment tax credits.

- BSE graduate, University of Maryland.

Although still at the above job, I am now seeking new opportunities and challenges. In light of your requirements, it would therefore be mutually beneficial for us to meet and discuss ways in which I would be an asset to your company.

Please let me know when such a meeting could be held at your earliest convenience.

Very truly yours,

LETTER 2

Your advertisement is an exact description of my background and capabilities in the educational endowments field.

A PhD graduate of Duke University, I have nine years experience in Public Service Administration, most of which has been in a supervisory/management capacity. Currently Director of a private foundation chartered to foster educational programs for gifted children, I head up a staff of eight people responsible for public relations, marketing, financial management, and operational activities.

As an example of my organizational abilities, two years ago I organized implementation of a computerized cross-indexing system that has proven to eliminate costly duplication of records, enabled a faster response to inquiries, and resulted in a 45 percent increase in productivity. Enabling us to reduce our staff by almost 30 percent due to attrition, this system has already more than paid for itself.

An integral part of my work is to raise funds from a variety of public and private sources and to maintain a constant dialog with financial institutions so that we can respond to our best advantage to the rapidly changing economic environment. In this regard, our capitalization has risen faster than expenses in recent years, despite a rapid growth in the number of projects we are handling.

I have also had considerable success in meeting with leading educators, publishers, and authors to get first-hand knowledge of needs and new developments. My familiarity with this area is therefore quite extensive.

It would be unfortunate if we did not meet to further explore mutual interests. My accomplishments are entirely documentable and I am prepared to discuss with you any nonproprietary aspects of my work.

Please let me know when we could meet at your convenience.

Very truly yours,

LETTER 3

I have seven years' secretarial experience, both in small and large offices. Having the ability to be an effective member of an office team, I am also willing and able to take responsibility and get the job done. Areas in which I excel are:

- Typing correspondence (65 wpm).

- Taking dictation, either from shorthand notes or tape.

- Taking and verifying telephone orders.

- Preparing, checking, and logging daily invoices.

- Operating Pneumographic word processor.

- Handling customer service functions, including referral to appropriate departments or individuals for processing.

- Preparing sales logs and maintaining running analysis of actual versus budgeted business levels.

Equally at ease in administration or inside sales, I am willing to change jobs only for an opportunity that would put my skills and experience to good use for many years to come.

I would welcome the opportunity to meet with you to discuss ways in which I could be an asset to your firm. To that end, I will call you within several days to determine when such a meeting could be held. If you prefer, please call me at the above number.

Very truly yours,

LETTER 4

Your advertisement describes a job that is a perfect match to my experience, education, capabilities, and career objectives.

A Registered Professional Engineer in four states, I have BSME and MME degrees from Carnegie Mellon University and twelve years' experience in the design and development of a wide variety of industrial noise control products, services, and systems.

I have personally engineered, sized, and field–tested industrial noise–control systems as diverse as HVAC silencers, machinery enclosures, power–plant silencers, anechoic chambers, and a host of others, including quieting systems for cooling towers, and jet–engine test stands. In addition, fans, machine tools, and gas–turbine engines are but a few of the many items of equipment I have redesigned for lower noise.

My papers on engineering acoustics have been published in Machinery Engineering, HVAC, In–Plant Digest, Urban Transit, and the proceedings of the American Institute of Acoustical Engineers. I have also written and delivered invited papers on noise control for several national trade associations.

Currently employed in New York by a major consulting engineering firm, I supervise a staff of four people who provide in–house acoustic design and analysis services for clients throughout the United States and Europe. My annual budgetary responsibilities have averaged well over $5 million and expenses have never exceeded budgets.

I would be happy to provide you with complete documentation of my education, professional status, accomplishments, and reputation. In light of your needs and my abilities and interests, we should meet to further discuss the matter in detail.

Please let me know when a meeting would be convenient for you.

Very truly yours,

LETTER 5

During my association with a heavy truck supplier, I have been active in a broad range of the heavy vehicular equipment business. Now seeking new opportunities in service support sales, my strengths are in the following areas:

- Service and display facility layout and organization.

- Organization, training, and management of maintenance personnel.

- Field repair and troubleshooting of operational malfunctions with long-haul highway trucks as well as with off-the-road vehicles.

- Complete familiarity with maintenance of pneumatic tooling, air compressors, diesel engines, gasoline engines, and related equipment.

- Negotiation and communications with customers, suppliers, and both union and nonunion personnel in various aspects of sales, purchasing, and service.

I have a total of eleven years' experience in this business, four of which have been with my current employer. The job described in your advertisement, however, would seem to offer long-range opportunities that are more in line with my career objectives.

The best way for me to prove my knowledge and abilities to you would be for us to meet and discuss in detail our needs relative to the specific equipment with which we are both so familiar. Accordingly, I will call your office next week for an appointment.

Please feel free to call me directly should you prefer to meet earlier.

Very truly yours,

LETTER 6

A graduate of Titan State College, I have more than seven years of responsible experience in all phases of customer service.

Specifically, I have been:

- Customer Service representative, XYZ Inc., Brooklyn, New York. Custom piping systems. Extensive customer telephone contact. Interfacing with management, salespeople, production personnel, accounting, and customers to coordinate the pricing, quotation, computer entry, scheduling, tracking, and routing of orders. 1986 to present.

- Customer Service Representative, D. Vintner & Sons, Lawrence, New Jersey. Pretzel manufacturer for commercial (retail chain) accounts throughout the greater metropolitan New York area. Order processing coordination of customers, sales, reps, and production.

- Customer Service Representative, Frivilo, Inc., Nanuet, New York. Alarm systems. Working with distributor sales force and house account customers. Quoting and entering orders, entering same on CRT, typing and maintaining logs and files, and coordinating schedules.

Although still employed at XYZ, I would welcome the opportunity to meet with you to further explore your needs and to answer any questions you might have. I will therefore call your office next Wednesday to determine when such a meeting can be scheduled at your earliest convenience.

Very truly yours,

LETTER 7

A graduate of Titan State College, I have more than eight years of responsible experience in all phases of customer service at:

- XYZ Inc., Brooklyn, New York. Manufacturer of custom piping systems. 1986 to present.

- D. Vintner & Sons, Lawrence, New Jersey. Pretzel manufacturer.

- Frivilo, Inc., Nanuet, New York. Alarm systems.

Skills and achievements pertinent to your needs that I have:

- Been responsible for the field service of commercial accounts throughout the greater metropolitan New York area.

- Coordinated sales, office staff, traffic, and accounting personnel as required for the efficient processing of orders.

- Interfaced with house accounts, distributors, retail chains, manufacturers, and sales staff, in addition to management personnel ranging from production foremen to the president.

- Extensive telephone contact.

- Quoted, entered, routed, and tracked customer activity manually and on computer systems.

Although still employed at XYZ, I would welcome the opportunity to meet with you to further explore your needs and to answer any questions you might have. Please let me know when such a meeting can be scheduled at your earliest convenience.

Very truly yours,

SOME DOS AND DON'TS

The following points summarize the keys to outstanding job-application letters:

DO

1. Put yourself in the shoes of each employer to whom you write a letter, and ask the question: What does this mean to me? If the question cannot be answered in a very affirmative manner, rewrite the letter.

2. Make certain that you have in each letter given facts which back up implications that you would be an asset in terms of efficiency, profitability, or effectiveness.

3. Gear your experience, as presented in a letter, to be as close as possible to the business needs of the employer to whom you are writing. If you are applying to a shoe retailer, talk about what you've done in that business, and not about your work in nuclear physics.

4. When responding to an ad, show how you meet the specifications listed. If you do not meet one or more of the specifications, imply that you do, or don't mention those particular items.

5. Describe your expertise and accomplishments in terms of figures and percentages which can quantify your value in a manner the employer can understand.

6. Use action words like *designed, established, directed, managed, implemented, built, supervised, organized, researched, achieved, accomplished, attained, succeeded, produced, constructed, conceived, conducted,* and so on.

7. Pay close attention to *what employers want.* When contacting targeted employers, send a different letter for each situation. Send a separate letter for each type business, for each business size, for each product or service, and for each type of job.

8. Send letters which are personalized for the intended reader. If you send form letters which look like form letters, an employer may infer that you couldn't take the time to write a separate application and that you may not be particularly interested in that company (or that you are just a lazy person).

9. Keep letters to one side of one sheet. Paragraphs should be no more than about eight lines so that important facts and implications do not get hidden in the midst of large paragraphs.

10. Be prepared to cover your tracks. Unless you can back up what you say, or unless it would be impossible for your statements to be disproved, don't say it.

11. Keep track of who is getting your letters. Even when you respond to ads, note each ad to which you send a letter. When a company advertises on successive days or weeks in a newspaper (or successive months in a trade journal), a good record-keeping system will help you know which bases you have already covered and what implications and statements you have made to which employer.

    Such records will also help when employers respond to your applications. If you can refer back to the ad as well as to the letter you sent to that particular employer, you will be able to intelligently deal with the situation.

12. Proofread. Finished letters should have all names spelled correctly and any mistakes detected and eliminated.

13. Be direct. If you beat around the bush, you are wasting space in your letter and taking up your reader's time. Look at this sentence:

    It seems to me, particularly in light of the qualifications stated in your advertisement, that my experience and capabilities put me in a unique position to meet your needs.

    Wouldn't it be far simpler to say: "I meet each of your stated qualifications."? If you think otherwise, go to the rear of the unemployment line.

14. Edit out *all* unnecessary words, phrases, clauses, and sentences. Look at the words which can be eliminated from these sentences:

    ~~It is clear that~~ we should meet to further discuss this matter.

    ~~I am writing to inform you that~~ your requirements are ~~almost~~ identical to my experience and capabilities.

    ~~In order to acquaint you with my rather unique capabilities,~~ the following achievements are ~~listed to provide you with~~ evidence ~~of the fact~~ that I meet ~~all of~~ your needs.

~~Inasmuch as you obviously want extensive experience in your field, you will note that~~ I have had similar jobs with two of your major competitors.

15. Avoid flowery adjectives, or phrases. Even simple adjectives are often unnecessary, and superlatives sound ridiculous.

Last year, I ~~successfully~~ exceeded quotas by ~~a fantastic~~ 61 percent.

My ~~superb~~ performance was the ~~very~~ best in the ~~entire~~ company.

Note that none of the words deleted from these examples is really missed. Before being deleted, these words merely got in the way of your message. Isn't each example more direct, more hard-hitting without those words?

Words such as *fantastic, magnificent, spectacular, superior, superb,* and so forth belong in movie advertisements and toothpaste commercials, not in job-application letters. The same goes for absolutes: *all of, every,* and *totally* usually sound out of place.

16. Avoid repetition of the same words and phrases in a letter. Get a thesaurus and a dictionary. If you find yourself repeating the same terms and expressions, find a different way to make your point.

17. Use active voice as opposed to passive. "I have processed an average of sixty-two applications per day for the past three years" sounds a lot better than "For the past three years, sixty-two applications have been processed by me each day." The second sentence is true, but by the time you finally get around to what *you* have done, the reader may lose interest.

18. Read your letters out loud. If possible, have someone else read them aloud so you can hear how they sound. Does the English sound contrived, stilted, or downright phony?

Would you use all those extra words in conversation?

19. Re-write until your letters are perfect.

20. Use proper English, correct spelling, and correct punctuation.

DON'T

1. Be shy. If you do not blow your horn, no one will do it for you. Learn to describe your accomplishments in glowing terms which will impress prospective employers.

2. Volunteer any information that will hurt your chances. Leave out salary, periods of unemployment, job titles of a more lofty nature than the job you are after, and even the year you graduated from college or high school. Employers will work backwards from the graduation year, calculate your age, and try to estimate your probable salary needs. Your letter, however impressive, may reach the circular file should the employer think that you're too old or too young.

   If you have worked in your field for five to ten years, it won't hurt to say so unless you know, with certainty, that the employer wants someone with much less or much more experience. If you are concerned about the wisdom of giving a specific number of years experience, don't. Concentrate entirely on showing how good you are.

3. Give your age. Any organization that claims to be an Equal Opportunity Employer must do so because of pressure from the government; whether they actually do not discriminate is another story entirely.

4. Identify present or former employers by name or by industry unless you can do so without jeopardizing your current job and without indicating that your experience is in a field quite unlike the business the prospective employer is in.

   A good experience "match" always helps, but lack of such a match probably does not hurt in nonmanagement jobs or when an employer's help-wanted ad emphasizes job skills instead of work background. See Chapter 8 for more details on experience criteria.

   If you want to establish industry/business experience credibility but don't want anyone asking about you, say that you have worked for "a major company in your field" or "a company similar to yours."

5. Give references in a letter. If pressed for references, give the names of people in whom you have complete trust and then only if you are certain that they will have only good things to say about you.

6. Present yourself as a jack-of-all-trades, unless you are applying to a company who is seeking a jack-of-all-trades. Otherwise, assume that prospective employers want specialists.

7. Plead for an interview, list personal problems, or discuss philosophical differences with your current boss. Employers may want to hire you, but they surely don't want to hire your problems.

8. Leave widows (one or two words alone on a line, usually at the end of a paragraph). You are too limited as it is, without such an inefficient use of space. When you see widows, rewrite by adding or subtracting words.

9. Describe your accomplishments in such a way that it could be inferred that they happened a long time ago. Avoid saying "When I was in the automobile business" or "prior to my current job". These expressions cannot help, and they may hurt in cases where the employer tries to read between the lines of your letter. You should give an accomplishment no tense as to when you did it, but only that you *did* do it.

10. Use cumbersome words or terms like *insofar as* or *inasmuch as*. You are writing a job-application letter, not a legal contract or a political treatise.

11. Say nasty things about current or past employers, and don't divulge company secrets. Present yourself as someone who is loyal and trustworthy and not the opposite.

12. Overqualify yourself. One of the most frustrating comments made to job candidates is "You're too strong for this job." What they really mean is that you're too old or too expensive for their tastes, or they would not expect you to be satisfied with the challenges of their job.

If you think you have too much experience for an advertised job, or if you suspect your age is working against you, don't say how many years you've worked in your field, but stress accomplishments and expertise in accordance with the job you're after.

You may be overqualified and challenges may be too tame for you, but why get to that point at the application stage? Get your foot in the door, get the interview, and then *you* decide if you're too strong.

13. Apply to a company for more than one job at one time. Decide which job you'd be most likely to get from a given employer and go after that job. If you write suggesting that you could fit a number of slots, your application may get a cool response.

14. Appear anxious. Employers like to hire people who are swayed by opportunities, not by the fact that they can't get anything else.

15. Forget that your letters must impress employers, not you, your friends, and your family. If any part of any letter does not get designed to impress employers, leave it out!

16. Keep on using the same letters unless you're getting results. If you are not getting calls and written responses in quantity within three to four weeks after sending out letters in quantity, try changing. Make your accomplishments stand out more, talk about your achievements in terms more akin to the bottom line, look more carefully for the ads on which you can realistically capitalize, re-reading Chapter 9.

If this is your situation, and you are convinced that you are going after the right ads for the right job, make some changes in your letters and keep trying. If you have the name, address, and telephone number of the people you have written, call them up after a couple of weeks; you have nothing to lose.

17. Waste space, when responding to an ad, by saying that you are interested in the job which was advertised. Of course you're interested; if you weren't, you wouldn't have responded.

18. Mention an achievement unless it is one which will impress employers. Changing jobs twice in two years to get a 40 percent pay increase is an accomplishment which will impress many people, but not employers.

19. Send pictures. Unless you are a very pretty girl and/or a model, your face will not help you get a job. Those who send photographs are interpreted as being on an ego trip.

20. Abbreviate. Spell out words.

21. Bury your reader in a sea of "I did this, I did that, I, I, I." Notice in the accomplishment examples in this book that the word *I* does not have to be used each time. Your letters, of course, are about you, and it is virtually impossible to eliminate the use of the word *I*. If you flood the page with that word, however, you may make yourself appear to be on an ego trip and your reader may want to avoid accompanying you.

In an opening or closing paragraph, instead of saying "I have been a circuit designer for six years", you can say "having worked in circuit design for six years" or "after six years as a circuit designer".

22. Send out handwritten letters.

23. Send letters which look like form letters. Your letters should look as if they were individually typed and signed, not mass-production printed.

24. Be shy about following up on your application. Responses to follow-up letters are very infrequent, so if you can, call the employer and politely ask whether your application has been received. If the answer is yes, ask if they have made any determination as to whether you are still under consideration.

As long as you do not demand information, you have virtually nothing to lose by asking the status of your application. If the employer has already decided you're not among the top candidates, it makes no difference if you are somewhat of a pest. If, on the other hand, the employer is interested in you, you probably won't hurt your chances as long as your follow-up does not show you to be particularly anxious or discourteous.

25. Send more than one application letter to the same employer. If your letter shows up more than once, or if you send two or more different letters to the same employer, you may be categorized as being possibly out of work and over-anxious, forgetful, or—in the case of two entirely different letters—somewhat of a liar.

26. Discuss why you're looking for a job. Chances are that your reasons, by themselves, probably will not help or strengthen your application. If you are out of work, disclosure of your reason for seeking employment will probably hurt your chances.

27. Send résumés.

11. Leading Inferences

Regardless of how good you really are, if the employer doesn't think you're good enough, you'll quickly be ruled out of contention. If that happens to you, it's nobody's fault but your own. At that point when you are first applying for a particular job, from what source does the employer get information about you? Who gives him the data from which he forms perceptions of how good you are and how well you might fit in?

You. You are the *only* source of information about you, and the employer knows only what you have told him. If he develops what you consider to be the wrong impression, it can only be because you have incorrectly assessed how that employer would interpret the information you supplied.

FRUITS OF YOUR LABOR

You have to present yourself to employers so that they can immediately see the value of your worth in terms meaningful to them. Those terms are always going to be very closely related to the reasons for the employer's existence, such as profitability, return on investment, efficiency in meeting budgets, or serving the public within funding allocations.

Can you prepare a list of accomplishments that shows how your work led directly to objectives being met? If not, surely you can show how your efforts led to increased efficiency, higher productivity, or a reduction in waste.

To illustrate the importance of showing the results of your achievement, suppose for the moment that your experience included a management job in which you were able to increase output while reducing the number of people on your staff. You could state the following facts about that experience:

> Reduced support staff by three people.
>
> Organized systems and procedures which added four units per week to the previous normal production rate.

Both of these statements could be entirely true, but an employer might read the above and say: What does this mean to me? or So what? The point is that you raise more questions than you answer. Three people out of how many? Six? Sixty? Six hundred? Similarly, four units out of how many? Five? Five thousand? Obviously, it makes a difference.

An improvement on the above might be:

> Increased production by 40 percent while reducing support staff by 25 percent.

Better, but still not as good as it ought to be. Had you been hired to reduce the staff? What were the results you were supposed to achieve? On what basis was your performance being judged? When you stop to think about it, the most important result in this case is higher productivity. The point is, however, that you have to stop and think about it; your reader may have neither the time nor the inclination to stop and think about anything. It is therefore up to *you* to make sure that your reader can get your point instantaneously.

The facts of your accomplishment should therefore be stated as follows:

> Conceived and implemented a personnel and procedures reorganization that resulted in a 40 percent increase in output with 25 percent fewer people: an 86 percent increase in productivity.

Unlike the previous attempts, this statement has a sledgehammer impact without your having to be the least bit egotistical. The reader would have to be extremely stupid if he or she could not see, from even a fleeting glance at this statement, that you are a very capable individual.

Whenever you state a fact or make a claim, remember this. Someone is going to hear or read that statement or claim and ask the question: What does this mean to *me?* When you write to an employer or when you compose a letter that will go to several employers in a group, your letter *must* answer that question. If you write to lawyers, you don't talk about how well you'd do in a butcher shop: you talk about how well you would do in a law office.

DON'T LIE—IMPLY

Facts can convince an employer that you are very good at the type of work you do, but an employer wants people who are more than good or even excellent at their work—employers want people who can fit in. Typically, therefore, an employer may ask: How would this candidate fit in *here*, with our company, in our business, with our people, our policies, our size, and our unique ideas?

On the basis of cold facts, you have no way of answering that question. You don't know the company, and you don't know their internal politics, their history, their prejudices, or their unique needs.

This, therefore, is the dilemma of every job-seeker: If you do nothing to convince the employer you will fit in, you lose control of what conclusions are drawn by the person who reads the letter. On the other hand, if you boldly state that you can solve all of the employer's problems, you will come across as being presumptuous, if not arrogant. Also, your believing that you are the perfect candidate doesn't make the employer agree with you.

The employer will agree with you only if he perceives that you meet his criteria, measure up to his values, and gratify his needs as related to the job at hand. All he has is your application, so he can't evaluate you on the basis of fact. He can only form impressions based on what you tell him and what his image is of what he wants. You obviously cannot think for the employer, but you *can* present selected information to him so that it would be virtually impossible for him *not* to draw just about any conclusion you want reached.

As mentioned briefly earlier, an *inference* is a conclusion reached on the basis of information which is known to be true or assumed to be true. When you contact an employer, the information you provide has to be assumed, by even the most cynical employer, as being possibly or probably true.

> In ten years of process-controls design management, I have successfully worked in both large and small companies on systems ranging from new concepts in automated energy conservation to nuclear-energy power systems.

Assuming for the moment that you are applying to a company in the process-controls design field, or one that needs expertise in that area, you have told them that you have been in the field for some time, that you have managed designs and programs, and that you would fit into both large and small operations. The reader would quickly infer that you would easily fit into an operation in which the demands were varied and involved high technology designs.

Successfully introduced five new products in four years.

In this case, you are implying a host of inferences: 1. that the success of the introductions was wholly or largely due to your own expertise; 2. that the expertise required to introduce those new products is similar to that required to do the same for the recipient of your letter; and 3. that the recipient of your letter could enjoy growth from new product sales if you were hired.

Perhaps none of the above is applicable; maybe the circumstances under which you operated were entirely different from those under which a new employer would let you work. Who knows? Not you and certainly not the prospective employer. All you can do is assume that you will be able to apply your expertise to the fullest. But more importantly, all the employer can do is to INFER that your expertise is fully transferable.

Implications can also help in other ways.

Published ten articles in eighteen months.

Someone who reads that fact would get the impression that you are quite prolific. Although the statement may be entirely true, it contains an implication that you not only published that much work in a short time, but that you also *wrote* that many articles in that time. You could have written the ten articles over a twenty-year period and published them in a flurry, or you could have written them in two weeks. The inference is up to the reader.

If an achievement occurred over a much longer period of time, you might be better off not mentioning that time period but rather concentrating on the scope of your writing.

Published ten different articles in twelve different trade and technical journals.

Invited lecturer before eight trade associations and three major universities.

The inescapable inference here is that you are a recognized expert in your field.

Plausibility

> Since becoming office manager, I was able to accomplish with six people the workload which previously required fourteen.

This sentence is BAD. It sounds too incredible, and it seems as if some other factors were involved in addition to the writer's capabilities. When you write a sentence like this, the reader may infer that you are either the world's greatest manager or the world's greatest liar. A far better approach would be to reword and add to the sentence as follows:

> Since becoming office manager, I have recommended and implemented use of systems, equipment, and techniques that enabled us to accomplish with six people the workload which had required fourteen.

This is plausible whereas the original was not. Whenever you exaggerate or make statements which may be interpreted as of doubtful validity, you give your reader an opportunity to question the truthfulness of everything else in your letter.

Avoid implying that you are being anything less than completely truthful in your letter. If you choose to imply certain things, you have to do it subtly so it is not detectable—at first glance—that the reader is being asked to draw an inference.

> There is no substitute for the right experience when it comes to furniture sales. In my case, that experience consists of ten consecutive years of exceeding goals and quotas.

This paragraph excerpt is precisely what an experienced furniture salesperson might say in the opening paragraph of a letter.

Interestingly, the same excerpt might be taken from a letter from someone who had never spent one minute in furniture sales. Read the words carefully. In the first sentence, the writer says that experience is important in furniture sales. The second sentence goes on to talk about the applicant's achievements. At no point does the letter say that those achievements were in furniture sales or that the ten years experience was in furniture sales. The writer's clever juxtaposition of words and phrases, however, clearly implies lengthy experience in that field. The reader of a letter containing the above excerpt will probably infer exactly what the writer has in mind.

In the above example, the writer feels that the "right" experience for this type of job can be obtained in other businesses. You may have the same opinion about your background with respect to the jobs for which you are applying. If you want to get your foot in the door without being eliminated even before the interview, you may wish to try this approach.

Referring back to Chapter 10, you will now be able to recognize some variations on the implication theme. Sentences like: "...sales manager for a company similar to yours..." clearly imply the same type of business, whereas such a contention was not directly stated.

Is this lying? It could be if you are grossly unqualified for the job or if your interpretation of similarities is beyond rational understanding. It could also be lying if you attempted to skirt the truth when confronted with a request for backup information in an interview. If you honestly feel that you are qualified to do the work involved in a particular job and you are prepared to explain yourself with strong arguments in an interview, use implications and let inferences work for you.

In the absence of information to the contrary, employers will infer that you are currently employed, that you have a good reputation, and that you are probably telling the truth. If you are not careful, however, employers can draw inferences that are not in your best interests:

- A letter that says you have had ten jobs in ten years may lead someone to infer that you are trouble with a capital T.
- A letter that is too vague may lead someone to infer that you have something to hide.
- Claims that are too extravagant may lead someone to infer that you are a liar.

Should these things happen to you, you have no one to blame but yourself.

CIRCUMVENTING

In Chapter 7 we discussed a technique for handling areas in which you may have shortcomings relative to an employer's hiring criteria. Called sidestepping, this technique is one in which you attempt to divert the employer's attention from areas you'd rather not discuss to those which are your strengths.

Circumventing is a cousin to sidestepping and may be used without changing the subject. In a letter format with appropriate implications, circumventing allows you to seemingly meet criteria without your having to make claims you cannot support.

Suppose you have only about half the ten years' experience specified by an employer for a particular job. If you feel you can handle the job, you'd be a fool not to apply. You can sidestep the issue of how much experience you have by simply not mentioning any number of years and not giving your age or year of graduation from high school or college, but that may give the employer the impression that you are purposely being too vague.

Circumventing length of experience can be handled by remembering that the ACBC letter format has four basic parts and that each part can talk about different jobs or the same job or your career as a whole. In the case of needing ten years' experience, you might say in the opening paragraph of your letter:

> Employed for the past four years by a major manufacturer in Chicago, I am in charge of providing programming assistance to all corporate offices and departments.

Then, in the middle of your letter, you could list an accomplishment such as:

> Completely familiar with FORTRAN IV scientific programming.

Near the end of your letter, you could state:

> Having changed employers only twice in ten years, I would not consider a new job unless it offered the level of opportunity described in your advertisement.

Hypothetically, you could have gotten into programming two or three years ago and been promoted to a supervisory job in computers after picking up the technology on your own and moving in from another department. Before you joined your current employer you might have been a rock singer.

These far-out suppositions are not in conflict with the three statements proposed above for your letter, but neither are they in conflict with the requirements of an employer who thinks he wants someone with ten years' experience in programming. Progressing from an introduction that describes your current job in that field to mention of several appropriate accomplishments, it will be quite natural for the reader to infer that the ten years you refer to were all in programming.

Another type of circumventing is applicable to employer requirements for particular educational degrees. If you do not have the degree and say you do, it might be embarrassing if you are asked to prove it. If, however, you have a degree in mechanical engineering while the employer wants an electrical engineering degree, the lack of the word *electrical* in one location may go unnoticed in a letter crammed with accomplishments in that field.

> Since getting my engineering degree from Harvard, I have worked in areas of increasing responsibility in electrical engineering and electronics design.

Even better, suppose you don't have any kind of engineering degree but you have life experiences that you believe qualify you for the job. Terrific! Go for it by circumventing.

> Since graduating from Harvard, I have worked in areas of increased responsibility in electrical engineering and electronics design.

Using implications and inferences to circumvent hiring criteria is effective, yet potentially hazardous to those job-seekers who get carried away. So face up to the fact that you will have to come clean at interviews. If all you are going to do is to use inferences as an excuse for lying, you are doing things the hard way. If the facts are clear and can be backed up at interviews, however, circumventing is a fine way for perfectly qualified job-seekers to make a good first impression despite ridiculous or unnecessarily rigid criteria.

Note: If you can't meet one or more known qualifications, don't mention those areas; concentrate on the qualifications you *do* meet.

OUT OF THE ORDINARY

Many of the above examples illustrate how implications work for people in management or other responsible jobs. The concept of using implications to enable employers to draw favorable inferences works equally well—if not better—if you have not had any kind of high-level jobs.

Suppose, as an example, that you've been a retail salesperson. Maybe 99 percent of the orders you rang up were for $20 or less. What, however, was the largest order you handled? $700? You could then say: Personally sold orders ranging from $20 to $700

Nothing humdrum about that! Saying that you averaged $20 a sale, however, is hardly impressive. Both ways of describing your experience are true, but which will help you more?

What have you done that can be described in ways which will mean most to employers? Did you make a suggestion to your boss, or did you "recommend and initiate implementation of procedures which increased efficiency by a factor of three"? Did you merely work someplace, or did you accomplish something while you were there? Maybe you learned or mastered certain procedures, or maybe you never took a day off in seven years. Whatever it was, say so and do it from the employer's point of view.

12. Fine Tuning

If you have learned nothing else in the preceding eleven chapters, you now know that job interviews, rather than being granted strictly on the basis of who is most likely to do the best work, will probably be restricted to people who are unlikely to require any training, demand top dollar, or do anything that might get the hiring boss in trouble.

This approach to selecting employees is designed to ensure that management can feel "better safe than sorry" about the people they bring on board. More important to our concerns here, however, it also results in a de facto preference for applicants who give the impression of having a narrow career focus. Even if you do outstanding work, your experience may be mistakenly judged to be too little or too varied to be useful, or too long ago to be currently applicable.

Alternatively, those of you who are well into your careers might be viewed negatively because of three perceptions: 1. that you may want too much money; 2. that you are too set in your ways to learn tricks that bosses think are unique to their needs; or 3. that you currently have such a great job that you are unlikely to be satisfied with the limited growth potential they can provide.

Such perceptions may be valid, but they are just as likely to be quite absurd. The following is a way to get the most out of tailoring your job application letters if your experience is too long, too short, or too fragmented in the minds of shortsighted employers.

IF YOU'RE JUST STARTING OUT

With no prior work background, you may have a difficult time finding a good job unless you have a degree in a specialty field, such as engineering, law, or business. Even then, you may have to start out in low-level jobs, and you might have to relocate if opportunities are limited within a practical commuting distance. But don't pack your suitcase yet. Regardless of whether you have been working for twenty years or for twenty minutes, you *can* convince employers that you are the "safest" person they can hire, but only if you go after the right jobs with the right strategies.

Being a neophyte to the job market does not mean that you should restrict yourself to going after entry level situations, nor should you try to get hired as a general manager the day after you graduate from high school or college. Seek out openings for which prospective employers would see you as a good candidate.

Look, for example, at "college grad" or other openings that offer training and ground-floor opportunities for growth. Be forewarned that "management trainee" is invariably a euphemism put into ads when employers want to hide the fact that what they really need are salespeople.

Do not lose sight of the reasons behind researching the companies for which you might work. The managers and the personnel people at these companies are well aware of what business they are in and whether they won or lost money last year. Telling them what they already know about themselves will serve no purpose but to demonstrate that you can read and write, which by itself won't be much help for most of the better jobs. Your reason for researching? To make a match between what someone wants and what you have to offer.

Whether a firm is advertising a specific job or you have identified it as having needs that may be a good match to your talents, skills, experiences, and interests, the procedure is exactly the same as described in the preceding chapters. Take things a step at a time, and begin by getting the prospective boss's attention in a way that will create a strong interest in wanting to meet you.

Start by identifying your strengths. How about your academic experiences and accomplishments? What subjects did you study to the greatest extent? At which did you excel? Did you have any connection with projects, reports, part-time jobs on or off campus, or research programs that might clearly demonstrate your potential? Think and you will no doubt come up with a long list of possibilities.

Your desire to get into the business or professional field in which an employer is offering opportunities may be viewed as a strength. Alternatively, your objective could be a specific type of work or relocation to a particular locale. In such cases, remember that what you want will be seen as irrelevant or negative unless it shows that you would be a good fit to the situation. If you feel obliged to state your goals, avoid blue-sky generalizations; be specific, be realistic, and say only what will help you to get consideration. Do not say anything about your objectives unless doing so will show that you are an excellent prospect who would be happy and fulfilled on the job.

Just because you have a short track record doesn't mean you have no track record. Okay, so you don't have years of job experience. How about months, weeks, days, or even hours? Remember, we're not writing résumés here, we're whetting appetites. How long you did something doesn't have to be disclosed unless you want it to be disclosed.

The circumstances under which you did something should be left out of the information you volunteer. This includes saying whether you were paid or unpaid, or did what you did part-time or full-time. Take another look at Chapter 7 and delete anything that might be construed as a negative in a job application letter. Say only what you did and how well you did it.

Look at your interests, your hobbies, your part-time jobs, your summer jobs, and your after-school jobs. If you helped fix a computer one Tuesday afternoon the winter before last, for example, you may have what an employer will consider relevant experience in computer repair, in circuit testing, or in electronics. Simply don't volunteer getting that experience on a single day a couple of years ago.

As someone who is just beginning a career, ask yourself, "Could I do this work now, without having to be retrained?" and "Can I make a case for being an ideal match to this employer's perception of a safe person to hire?" If you can back up your claims with a credible story, and if you can do what you say you can do, summon up your guts and go for it!

IF YOU HAVE GAPS IN YOUR WORK HISTORY

As pointed out on page 75, employers like a consistent employment record. If you have not been working for some time, they may fear that your knowledge is out of date; that you haven't kept up with changes in the equipment, laws, technologies, or other factors that affect the type of work you do; that you would have difficulty re-acclimating yourself to the rigors of a structured workday; or that there may be something wrong with you.

Don't let these stupidities get to you. The people who are in a position to hire you may be afraid of their own shadows when it comes to hiring. No matter how irrational they may be, you have to let them think that you are playing by their rules. But just because they're not functioning with a full deck doesn't mean that you can't have a few aces up your sleeve.

Using conventional résumés may put you in the position of having to explain why you weren't employed during certain time periods, so leave out the years when you were at previous jobs. If you are working now, you could give your history only for that job by saying something like:

> "(fill in name of job) for (fill in name of company) at (fill in name of city and state). Since (fill in year)."

Unless giving your complete work history helps, don't say when you were where. Concentrate on what you *have* done, not on what you haven't done recently. In the event that you haven't been employed in five or ten years, or if you took off a few months or even a few years to raise a family or to contemplate the secrets of the universe, you can then offer yourself on an even basis with others who have been on someone's payroll all along.

The same applies if you decided at one point to travel, to study on your own, or to take time off to rethink your goals while you support yourself by working menial jobs. There's nothing wrong with those activities, but to the typical corporate mentality, an adult who does anything but work in accordance with a conventional career path is likely to be looked upon as undesirable. This is particularly true if you are or have ever been out of work. You may have nothing to be ashamed of, but you are asking for trouble if you volunteer information on bouts with unemployment.

By now, however, you should know better than to fall into that trap; if information has even the slightest chance of being looked on negatively, don't use it!

IF YOU'RE A SEASONED PRO WITH A VARIED BACKGROUND

The mature, experienced applicant has a lot to offer on paper; particularly if he or she has a broad-based work record. A veteran of ten, fifteen, or even more years in the thick of things would be highly prized if hiring practices were controlled by logic.

Unfortunately, most hiring decisions are based on fear. There are exceptions, but in the minds of too many bosses, the inexperienced candidate will demand less pay, require less training, and be less likely to threaten the current power structure. Such thinking may be the ultimate in stupidity, but it is the conventional wisdom that prevails when many jobs are filled.

To be sure they don't get caught up in that nonsense, job-seekers with a great deal of experience must slant their application letters so that what might be ridiculously looked upon as "too much" experience is not apparent. In this regard, which of the following is more truthful? Which has more negatives?

    a. "more than five years experience"

    b. "twenty years experience"

Twenty is more than five, so both are equally truthful. In most cases, however, version b will bring with it a negative connotation whereas version a will not be inferred to mean anywhere near twenty. If a particular employer is known to want twenty years experience, on the other hand, version b should be used.

With conventional résumés, the more experience you have, the deeper a hole you dig for yourself. With the job application letters described in Chapters 10 and 11, however, a great deal of experience need not hurt at all. You can pick and choose which aspects of your career to include, which to save for another day, and which to present only after careful wording that eliminates all negatives.

When you list an employer, an industry, or a profession with which you have had experience, readers will not know whether that experience was gained one or thirty years ago. The only exception is when you want to give the impression that a job or an achievement is recent, in which case you should list that item first. There, it will have the greatest prominence. And, if it shows a title no lower than you have had at other times, the item listed first will by many people be assumed to be the most current.

FILL IN THE BLANKS

No matter what your situation, the simplest way to organize and design your job application letters is to construct a skeleton that can be varied to suit virtually any need. When presenting your academic history, for exmple, you can present yourself as:

A graduate of (fill in name of school)

A (fill in year of graduation) of (fill in name of school), or

A recent graduate of (fill in name of school)

The first example gives no clue as to when you got your degree. Depending on the year you insert, the second shows exactly how much experience you have, and the third says nothing about the length of your experience. Each is truthful, yet each has a different slant you can use to your advantage depending on your best guess as to what will be of greatest interest to the prospective employer.

Another use for filling in the blanks is to dole out information only to the extent that it helps you get a foothold. Some of the sample letters shown previously in this book do not list the names of current or previous employers, but the key in all these strategies is to use what will work best for you, not to go by some rigid formula. If you are applying to a leader in an industry and you are familiar with that field, you might do well to identify where you have worked or are working. Accordingly, you could present one aspect of your background as:

— Accountant at _____ in _____

where two possibilities are:

- — Accountant at the Mugwump Iron Works in Wesley Hills, New York.

  or

- — Accountant at a major structural fabricator in a suburb of New York City.

Or, suppose you had been in your current job since 1980. You could then describe that aspect of your career by saying:

- — Accountant at the Mugwump Iron works in Wesley Hills, New York _____.

where you might have three choices for filling in the blank:

a. since (fill in year).
b. for more than (three, five, or ten as appropriate) years
c. no entry

Filled in, your options would be:

- — Accountant at the Mugwump Iron Works in Wesley Hills, New York since 1980.

- — Accountant at the Mugwump Iron Works in Wesley Hills, New York for more than five years.

- — Accountant at the Mugwump Iron Works in Wesley Hills, New York.

Can you see how these are different? The first clearly shows you to have senior-level experience, whereas the second, although equally truthful, implies experience, but not what might be construed as "too much" experience for certain jobs. The last choice, which says nothing about how long you worked for Mugwump, would be good if you did not want to disclose the timing or sequence of that job.

Let's construct the opening paragraph of a job application letter given the following facts about a hypothetical job applicant:

- Graduate degree last year from the Joule School of Management and Economics at Central Connecticut University
- Graduate degree is an MBA in Marketing
- Undergraduate degree, BS in Business Management, earned eight years ago, from Armarc College
- Work history after graduating Armarc:
  - Two years as financial planner for Garson & Stark, investment bankers, Cincinnati, Ohio
  - Four years as marketing manager for Planhurst Industries, aerospace electronics group, Los Angeles, California
  - Two years as operations manager for Planhurst Industries, office products group in Houston, Texas

An appropriate job application letter for this person might start with an opening paragraph skeleton that says:

$$\underline{\quad 1 \quad} \text{ of } \underline{\qquad\qquad 2 \qquad\qquad} \text{ Central Connecticut University,}$$
$$\underline{\qquad\quad 3 \qquad\quad}. \text{ My career includes } \underline{\qquad\qquad 4, 5, 6 \qquad\qquad}:$$

Using everything we have discussed to this point, let's see what might be inserted into 1, 2, 3, 4, 5, and 6. Here are some possibilities:

1a. A graduate

1b. An MBA graduate

1c. A recent graduate

1d. A recent MBA graduate

1e. A (fill in year) graduate

1f. A (fill in year) MBA graduate

1g. An honors graduate

2a. no entry (No entry for option 2. See the example that follows.)

2b. the Joule School of Management and Economics at

3a. I also have a BS degree in Economics from Armarc College

3b. I have a Masters Degree in Business Administration and Marketing.

3c. I have a Masters Degree in Business Administration and Marketing. I also have a MS degree in Finance from Armarc College.

4a. having been

4b. more than five years

4c. four years

4d. six years

4e. eight years

4f. strong

4g. no entry

5a. no entry (Nothing entered for option 5; see the next example.)

5b. marketing and operations management experience:

5c. marketing management experience:

5d. operations management experience:

5e. financial, operations, and marketing management experience:

5f. financial and operations management experience:

5g. financial and investment planning experience:

6a. no entry

6b. as follows

Let's look at a few of the many possibilities. One is:

> A graduate of Central Connecticut University. I have a Masters Degree in Business Administration and Marketing. My career includes having been:

No clue is given as to the applicant's year of graduation, and only one aspect of the applicant's academic background is given. This opening would be appropriate for a job that is heavily into marketing and might be tough to get for someone with what might be perceived as little or no practical experience. If, on the other hand, the employer were known to be seeking a relatively recent graduate whose background were heavier in management, economics, and finance, a better approach would be to say·

> A recent MBA honors graduate of the Joule School of Management and Economics at Central Connecticut University, I also have a BS degree in Finance from Armarc College. My career includes having been:

Still another possibility would be to maximize the applicant's strength by being vague about the year of graduation and by emphasizing the work experiences that would be of interest to a prospective employer:

> An MBA honors graduate of the Joule School of Management and Economics at Central Connecticut University, I also have a BS degree in Finance from Armarc College. My career includes more than five years financial, operations, and marketing management experience as follows:

Want to go a little heavier on the financial side? No problem:

> An MBA honors graduate of the Joule School of Management and Economics at Central Connecticut University, I also have a BS degree in Finance from Armarc College. My career includes more than five years financial and investment planning experience as follows:

If the employer wants only operations and financial management experience, yet another combination can be used:

> A recent MBA honors graduate of the Joule School of Management and Economics at Central Connecticut University, I also have a BS degree in Finance from Armarc College. My career includes strong financial and operations management experience as follows:

Which is best? That depends upon the job, the employer, and what that employer wants.

In describing the applicant's financial experience, the next section of the letter could be written in numerous ways, one of which is:

> — Garson & Stark, Investment Banking, Cincinnati, Ohio.
> _____7, 8, 9, 10, 11_____.

where the options are:

> 7a. Specialized in
>
> 7b. Managed
>
> 7c. no entry
>
> 8a. government securities
>
> 8b. corporate bonds
>
> 8c. mutual funds
>
> 8d. any other financial instrument

8e. any combination of 8a through 8d

8f. no entry

9a. and

9b. no entry

10a. pension funds

10b. personal asset management

10c. retirement planning

10d. leveraged buyout financing

10e. any other financial planning need

10f. any combination of 8a through 10e

10g. no entry

11a. Established and maintained CEO-level contacts throughout Ohio, Michigan, and Indiana.

11b. Developed seventy million dollars of investment accounts in two years.

11c. Managed a portfolio worth in excess of a hundred million dollars.

11d. no entry

The many ways to present this information include:

— Garson & Stark, Investment Banking, Cincinnati, Ohio.

— Garson & Stark, Investment Banking, Cincinnati, Ohio. Specialized in government securities.

— Garson & Stark, Investment Banking, Cincinnati, Ohio. Leveraged buyout financing.

— Garson & Stark, Investment Banking, Cincinnati, Ohio. Managed pension funds.

— Garson & Stark, Investment Banking, Cincinnati, Ohio. Specialized in corporate bonds and personal asset management.

— Garson & Stark, Investment Banking, Cincinnati, Ohio. Managed a portfolio worth in excess of a hundred million dollars.

The remainder of this applicant's experience was gained at Planhurst Industries — four years as marketing manager in aerospace electronics, two years as operations manager in office products. These can be presented separately or together as shown below:

— Planhurst Industries, _____12, 13_____.

12a. marketing management, Aerospace Products Group, Los Angeles

12b. operations management, office products group

12c. marketing and operations managment

12d. no entry

The applicant can emphasize experience in specific industries or no particular industry at all. If either 12a or 12b is chosen, the next series of options can be used to further slant the Planhurst experience as may be appropriate:

13a. Established and maintained contacts throughout NASA, the aircraft industry, and the defense electronics industry.

13b. Promoted the sale of aerospace electronics microprocessors to all major airframe and shuttle program vendors.

13c. Familiar with all government space and defense agency personnel who influence space program purchase decisions and specifications.

13d. Familiar with government space and defense agency personnel who influence microprocessor purchase decisions and specifications.

13e. Managed the marketing, sales, design, and production of furniture and accessories for five million square feet of office space throughout the United States and Canada.

13f. Increased profits by 62% in two years on a sales increase of 39%.

13g. Managed two hundred fifty people in nineteen offices and factories in seven states.

13h. no entry

Three of the many possibilities here are:

— Planhurst Industries, marketing management, Aerospace Products Group, Los Angeles. Familiar with government space and defense agency personnel who influence microprocessor purchase decisions and specifications.

— Planhurst Industries, operations management, office products group. Managed two hundred fifty people in nineteen offices and factories in seven states.

— Planhurst Industries. Promoted the sale of aerospace electronics microprocessors to all major airframe and shuttle program vendors.

At the end of your letter, the closing paragraph could be:

Even though I am still employed ____14____, I would welcome the opportunity to meet with you and answer any questions you might have. _____15_____.

where the choices are:

14a. no entry

14b. by (fill in name of current employer)

15a. Please let me know when such a meeting can be scheduled at your earliest convenience.

15b. I will therefore call your office next (fill in day of week) to determine when such a meeting can be scheduled at your earliest convenience.

See how easy it is?* You don't have to go through any rigorous procedures, and you can easily combine filling in the blanks with stressing strengths of potential interest while leaving out information that might be thought negative or irrelevant. In the case just described, for example, the applicant's investment company background might be deleted to make a highly focused case for expertise in specific management areas. Or, it might be kept in for the benefit of an employer who indicates an interest in marketing, operational, *and* financial management experience.

The bottom line is that a little advance planning with a "fill in the blanks" letter design can dramatically increase the speed with which you can customize first-class job application letters in quantity. When you apply for several diverse jobs simultaneously, you won't have to create a new letter for every situation, and yet all the implications you need will be right at your fingertips. As a result, you'll be able to respond faster and more effectively than would be the case if you had to customize each letter from scratch.

---

*Easy but not foolproof. You still have to check each finished letter to be sure that your punctuation is correct and that the end result is not badly phrased.

13.
Controlling the Interview

The more interviews you have, the better your chances of landing a good job. If you have properly applied the concepts on the previous pages, you should, within a few weeks, be getting a number of calls and letters asking you to come in for interviews.

It is the goal of the employer in the interview to size you up: to evaluate you as a potential employee. You may not get an offer during the first interview, but if you make a good impression, the employer will try to see that you leave with a good feeling in case they decide in your favor.

You also have a goal: you have to sell yourself. You'll form various impressions of the interviewer or the job; fine. File these impressions away until later. For now, you must sell, sell, sell until you are convinced that you have made a good impression. Then you can size up the employer and get a feel for whether you would like to work there.

CONTROL

To meet your priorities, you have to make sure that neither the interview nor the interviewer gets in your way. As long as you meet your goals (selling yourself), the interview will be successful. If you have made a good impression, the employer will perceive that he or she is talking to a winner. If, on the other hand, the employer meets his goal (determining if you are his potential employee) and you do *not* meet yours, you will have squandered an opportunity.

You have no choice. You *must* control the action so that the interview stays on course and you continue to find out more and more about the hiring criteria and convince the employer that you are that elusive ideal candidate.

Controlling the interview is a matter of directing the conversation toward topics that emphasize your strengths while steering it away from topics that might emphasize your shortcomings. Since interviews are relatively short meetings (an hour or less), you don't have time to indulge in complicated ways of dealing with people. You need a simple, direct, and relatively quick method of getting the information you need so you can make a good impression that is rapidly and firmly established.

Fortunately, such a method exists. It's called *asking*.

When in Doubt, Ask

In Chapter 7, we discussed the fact that when you are in doubt as to whether to include certain information in your application, you should leave it out. The same is true in interviews, except that when in doubt in an interview, you can always ask for more clues.

First of all, you can ask an interviewer to tell you about his functional hiring criteria. "Do you have a written job description I might look at?" is a question that is not at all out of line, and with many interviewers, will be taken as a sign of proper prudence on your part. If there is nothing in writing, the interviewer will either start to tell you about those criteria or ask you why you asked. If questioned, you can be ready: "I don't necessarily need a *formal* job description; I really just want to make certain I understand what you want and what results you're looking for from the person you hire."

If you can carry off that short bit of conversation, you will have made it clear that you are interested with prudence, not anxiety that might be pushing you to accept anything that comes along. Also, by saying that you don't necessarily need a formal job description, you will have implied that you are capable of functioning without written instructions. These points are to your benefit, but the important thing is that the employer will now start talking about criteria and you can respond in kind by emphasizing your strengths and the results you can achieve.

Asking for hiring criteria can also serve purposes other than getting information. For example, one purpose might be to change the subject to one *you* want to talk about. As the employer is describing some routine aspect of the job, you can politely interrupt during a pause and say: "That's interesting ... Have you ever heard of (name a related topic, procedure, or operating method you'd like to talk about)?" If "Have you ever heard of ..." doesn't sound right to you, you can use "Have you ever tried ...?" You *will* get a response, either "Yes" with an opinion or "No." If the answer is no, you have an opening to talk about something that you have done of merit. Of course, if you use some uncommon name for your procedure, you can be certain that the person with whom you are talking will have never heard of it.

Questions can also help you draw out the employer's personality and—in the process—his preferences for the characteristics you would have to display to get the job. Asking for a rundown of qualifications is liable to elicit a response that the interviewer has on the tip of his or her tongue, but don't settle for that. Make him think and see what he comes up with off the top of his head. The question "What characteristics would you *not* want in the person you hire?" will force him to look at the job from a reverse vantage point, and—in doing so—perhaps cause him to give you a gut reaction that is more open than a routine listing of characteristics he says he wants. Pose this question *after* discussing the job description and, if asked why you have made such a request, be honest and say that you are only trying to gain insight into what is required. Should the interviewer have a pained or quizzical expression on his face, don't press the matter; say "Okay, let me rephrase; what personality characteristics would you think would be most useful to whoever gets this job?"

Another way to discover the stuff the employer is made of is to ask on what basis your performance would be judged. An indication of what you are expected to do to be well thought of or to get increases in salary or to earn bonuses should tell you not only how to answer questions but also whether this is the kind of outfit you'd want to work for.

For jobs involving any degree of independent responsibility, consider asking: "I realize that it's difficult to talk in specifics, but in a general sense, what activities would I be expected to carry out on my own as opposed to getting your approval?" This is a perfectly legitimate query from someone evaluating a job possibility. Do you get an open answer that is reasonably well defined, or do you get a look that implies that you've got a lot of nerve asking such a question? A vague response following that kind of look may be indicative of a boss who doesn't like the idea of delegating responsibility on a planned or organized basis. In context with your other impressions from the rest of the interview, the answers you get to these questions will give you some hard thinking to do should you get an offer.

Another use for asking questions is to blunt other questions from the employer. Imagine walking into an office, receiving a warm greeting, shaking hands, getting comfortable in a nice chair, and being asked a question like: "What do you think you can do for us?"

If you are prepared, you will be ready with: "That's hard to say unless I know more about your operation. If you would describe your needs, I'd be glad to tell you if and how I could meet them." This type of response can also be used whenever you're not quite sure what the interviewer is getting at. A favorite question of employers is: "What do you consider your primary weaknesses?" This is a loaded question because in many cases it is asked only to see how you respond under pressure to a potentially embarrassing question. Don't let this question throw you. Say that you don't think you have any weaknesses as far as the job is concerned, or turn the tables by responding with: "I don't know that I have any real weaknesses in this area, but let me put your question in perspective. What would you consider to be a primary weakness?" You *will* get an answer, and it may even provide you with some interesting insight into hidden hiring criteria.

REMEMBER THE RULES

All the motivational rules for job applications are also valid for job interviews: keep the employer's point of view in mind at all times, sell yourself on the basis of positive attributes, avoid negatives, appeal to values, meet needs, and imply whatever you can back up if asked.

Following the rules also means remembering that you want the employer to leave the interview thinking that he has gained from the experience. Gained what? A great deal of confidence in someone who seems to be the best candidate available. Even better, the interviewer should leave the meeting thinking that the search is over. He thinks he wins, if you want the job; you think you win, if he wants you.

TELEPHONE INTERVIEWS

Opening a telephone application was discussed in Chapter 9. The next step is to keep the conversation going and becoming an interview. As soon as the employer acknowledges that he has a bona fide opening, but before he starts to ask about you, you should ask about the job. You obviously cannot be shown a written job description over the phone, but you can ask for required skills, level of responsibility, and other hiring criteria. After that, your interview is off and running.

Get the Facts

Whether you call an employer or an employer calls you in response to an application you have already sent in, make certain you get the correct spelling of the name of the person with whom you are speaking. If you get a surprise call from a potential employer, you may even want to ask the caller to please hang on a minute while you get pencil and paper. So what if you actually have those items in front of you? The break may be helpful to you, particularly if you were concentrating on something else when the call came or if you had to run to pick up the phone. Use a few seconds here to get your mind in focus.

If the caller indicates that the call is in reference to an ad to which you have responded, ask him (or her) to refresh your memory about the ad and specifically what it said—even if you have it at your fingertips. This gives you an opportunity to be told what the employer wants before you've said anything about yourself. Do not, however, let the caller get away with merely reciting the words in the ad; press for more information. You could, for instance, say something like: "Yes, I remember that ad. Can you tell me more about the job?"

This open-ended question will perhaps cause the caller to immediately try to sell you on the job as a justification for calling you. The caller may be quite expert at this, however, and answer your question with another question, such as "Is there anything specific that you'd like to know?"

If that happens, you can have your own questions ready to ask: "What is the scope of the job?" "What responsibilities would I have?" "To whom would I report?"

Avoid Controversial Subjects

Steer clear of discussing religion, politics, foreign affairs, or any topic which may involve strong feelings on your part or on the part of the interviewer. Human nature being what it is, you may find yourself in disagreement with the interviewer about some topic which is totally unrelated to your interview or the job. Why get the interviewer to disagree with you on anything?

If your religious beliefs are attacked by the interviewer, that's one thing. If you get embroiled in a discussion over some controversial topic unrelated to the job and the interview, however, you are foolishly introducing disharmony into a meeting which should have resulted only in the two of you agreeing.

Be Yourself

Unless you have had considerable acting experience, you are going to have problems during interviews if you try pretending to be anyone but yourself. Putting your best foot forward is one thing, but putting forward a foot that isn't even yours is pointless. If you were to succeed on that basis, the person others perceive you to be might get hired, but the person you really are wouldn't be able to function. There's a great deal to concentrate on in an interview and you will only distract yourself if you go too far astray and have to constantly worry about your act.

Also while being yourself, remember that people have eyes in the front of their heads. That's to keep us looking forward, not backwards. People are not perfect, and occasionally do screw up.

You are no different. You can't rationally conduct an interview and worry about whether you just said something wrong or if you may say something else wrong. If you make a mistake, you make a mistake. That doesn't mean that it is a critical mistake, but even if it is, forget it. There will be other days and other interviews.

> "Is this a newly created job or would I be replacing someone?" "What is the growth potential on this job?" Or, if appropriate to your situation, "Are there others at your company doing the same kind of work?"

These questions do not have specific, short answers, but rather require an explanation of the employer's situation and wants.

Don't ask all of these questions at once, but just enough to keep the conversation going and to give you a pretty good feel for what is needed.

Sell Yourself

Once you've asked these questions you will have a definition of the employer's wants before you have said a thing. When you do say something, you can frame your statements and responses toward indicating that *you* are precisely the right person.

A question can also be used to show your familiarity with a subject as well as to get more information from the interviewer: "Does your data system use on-line or batch processing?" "Do you prefer manual or automatic controls?" Whichever answer you get, you'll know the direction in which you'll have to show yourself as being an expert.

When you are asked a question, by all means respond, but answer without volunteering information that may hurt you. Suppose, for example, a caller says: "I see you say that you have worked extensively in our field." Although that statement is not a question, it is designed to provoke a response, and—human nature being what it is—it can all too easily bring on a case of foot-in-mouth disease for applicants. Most job-seekers would not be able to resist going into a long dissertation at this point, identifying every employer they've had in the field, the complete history of employment at each job, and what they did.

Wrong.

The lengthy response is wrong because you would be volunteering information before you know whether that information will help or hurt you. You may have had too many jobs to suit the interviewer, you may specialize in concepts with which the employer is not familiar, you may have had more responsible jobs than the employer is thinking of at the minute, and you may even talk too much.

The opposite approach: "Yes, that's right" is also wrong; it's too short and uncommunicative. To each individual question (or statement obviously requiring a response), give an answer that is both direct and relevant, but that is also as short and brief as possible while providing the interviewer with a little more information. A good answer might therefore be: "Yes, that's correct. I've had similar jobs with both Amalgamated Freight and General Gas."

This response is not curt, not terse, and not vague, and yet it is also not damaging to you in any way. You have, of course, disclosed additional information not contained in your application letter, but you have done this at your convenience. If the employer wants to find out about your employment with either or both of these companies, let him ask.

In this regard, if the caller asks about a particular subject, talk on that subject only. Before responding, ask yourself: "What does this person want me to say?" "What answer will do the best job of selling me?" When you give your response, do *not* run off at the mouth.

If there is a lull in the conversation at a time when you think the caller is waiting for you to say more, ask another question. Get the caller to talk, to tell you about their situation. At that point, you can come back with additional information which supports your claim that you would fit in quite well with their needs.

One way to do this is to ask a question which has already been answered. You can even do this by making a statement which *you* have designed to provoke a response: "By the way, you did say that this job involves budgetary control, didn't you?" Chances are the interviewer will respond by expanding on that aspect of the job. This gives you an ideal opportunity to expand on your expertise in that area.

Obviously, you use this approach as a lead-in to areas you want to talk about relative to your strengths. Do *not* raise any points in a manner which might indicate that you are weak on a particular portion of the job, or would not be interested in certain aspects of what they are talking about. There's plenty of time for that later. Right now, concentrate on selling yourself. Once they're sold on you, *then* you may be able to negotiate yourself into a better position and, if not, you can always turn them down.

It should go without saying, but don't ask your questions as if you were a prosecutor and the interviewer a defendant. Your tone of voice should be that of a person asking questions out of genuine interest.

Sound Relaxed

Whether you actually are relaxed may be one thing, but you must sound relaxed over the phone, and you must respond as if you are a self-confident person who is anything but arrogant or cocky.

It is impossible to prepare a script which will work in all interview situations. You have to take the attitude that if you goof, you goof and that's all there is to it. As you get more interviews, you will become more expert at handling yourself in these situations.

Suppose someone calls in response to a letter you have sent to a targeted employer. What do you do? Ask questions. Of course you remember writing to them, but before you go into more details on your background, say that you assume that they are calling because they have a need you may be able to fill. Get them to talk about that need, *then* tell them about yourself relative to meeting that need.

IN-PERSON INTERVIEWS

An in-person interview is one of the two hurdles you have to clear; the other is getting the job.

Before you go, make certain that you are properly dressed. Wear clothes which would be appropriate for the job you are seeking. Regardless of what you wear, make sure it's clean and neat. If you look like a slob, employers will tend to think that you think and act like a slob, an impression that's bad unless you've happened to find an employer who has advertised for someone to become the corporate slob.

If the interview requires you to incur any significant travel expenses, ask in advance whether the employer will reimburse you for those expenses. If the answer is no, don't go to the interview unless you are willing and able to spend the money on the chance that you'll get the job. If you are after any kind of professional job, it is customary for employers to reimburse candidates for interview travel expenses, but you have to ask anyway. If an employer will not reimburse a professional job candidate for travel expenses, that employer should be considered a bad prospect.

Application Forms

Many employers will ask you to fill out an application form, even before the interview. Typically, these application forms have spaces for you to fill in information regarding when you've worked for which employer, salaries, reasons for leaving, job titles, names of supervisors, and so forth. Rarely do these forms leave space to list your career accomplishments or to list achievements which show how good you are. Worst of all, many agencies and companies use one standard form, and all applicants are asked to fill out that form, regardless of whether they seek employment as executive vice-president or night watchman.

For management jobs, jobs with a high creativity content—such as advertising, engineering, or fashion design—or for jobs requiring specialized skills or a specific type of personality, application forms will only get in your way. To get these jobs, you have to sell yourself on the basis of your capabilities, your skills, and achievements that illustrate what you can do. Application forms not only rarely ask for this information, they invariably leave no space for it.

Many employers use the responses on the form as a basis for asking questions at the interview. Without that form you have a better chance of controlling the pace and content of the interview, but if asked to fill in the blanks, do so without hesitation.

But fill the form out to your advantage. Do *not* list the names of current or past supervisors unless you are positive that, if contacted, they will neither jeopardize your current job nor ruin your chances of getting future jobs. Other information not to be provided includes current or past salaries and your present income requirements. If you are currently employed, it would also be prudent to make it clear that you do *not* want your employer contacted about you.

Might an employer discriminate against you because of your age? Do not fill in information about your date of birth, years of graduation from high school and college, ages of children, and so forth. Be leery also of categories on application forms in which you are asked to list clubs and associations to which you belong. This information may be used to determine your religion or your beliefs in other areas that have nothing to do with your job.

Don't worry about handing in a form with a number of blank spaces. If the interviewer is disturbed about blank spaces, he can always ask for the information during the interview. An employer whose legitimate concern is your ability to do a job will not be upset if you don't list hobbies or you leave blank any other area that has nothing to do with your functional qualifications.

So much for negatives. If you know, *without any doubt*, that the name of a former or present supervisor will help, write it down! The same goes for indicating your age, religion, affiliations, and anything else that will help make a good impression.

Also on the positive side, do you always do everything people tell you to do? So they don't ask for achievements . . . so what? Put achievements in anyway! Add the same material you have in the B part of your application letter. Write as small as you can so as to say as much as you can about your accomplishments.

Then we come to the touchy subject of past or current unemployment. There is nothing to be gained by telling an employer that you were out of work for eight months five years ago, but he might ask about gaps in your employment record if you have filled out his forms in such a way as to show gaps. Why show gaps? Either do not put down when you started or left an employer, or just show the year without indicating the month. If you have been out of work for some time, can you make a case for your being self-employed?

If you are currently unemployed, you have three choices:

- You can indicate that you are now unemployed. Depending upon the type of job you're seeking, the length of your unemployment, and the reasons for your unemployment (combined with what your last employer would say about you if contacted), this may keep you from getting a job. If you've been out of work for a year and you're seeking a responsible position, prospective employers will tend to think that there is something wrong with you.

- You can say that you have been self-employed at some business and that you have decided working for yourself isn't for you. If that's true, fine. If it is a fabrication, be prepared to pay the potential consequences if you're found out. Also, be prepared to ask a good friend to substantiate your claims; the employer will probably want a reference who knows your work during your period of self-employment (as well as others relative to your prior jobs).

- You can say that you left to go with a company which has since folded. Again, this is fine if it's true, but it may cause all kinds of problems if it isn't.

The final choice is entirely up to you. These alternates are presented only because job-seekers must eat and support families. Only you can determine the extent to which your needs should override your sense of ethics. If and when you decide to re-write history in order to get a job, however, make sure that you can back up everything you say.

Should you be asked to fill out an application form *after* an interview, supply whatever information is requested, consistent with what you said in the interview, but nothing more. If they want more, they'll ask for it.

Be Prepared

There is no way you can go into an interview with a script, but you can be prepared. This means knowing the going salary in your field, memorizing a brief list of questions, being armed with one or two short stories that illustrate your merits, and also knowing how to answer the kinds of questions you are likely to be asked.

Immediately after you complete an interview, make careful notes and write down whether there were any aspects of the interview for which you felt unprepared. Then determine what you should have done. Next time you'll do better, and the time after that you'll do even better.

Bring Evidence

Feel free to bring evidence of your expertise, but don't show the secrets or property of your current or past employers. Photographs, articles, reports, publications, small samples are all okay as long as your material can show, with a reasonably rapid series of glances, that you're as good as you say you are.

Eyeball to Eyeball

In an interview, greet the interviewer with a firm, but not bone-crushing, handshake. Sit and stand erect. Do not chew gum, smoke, or fidget with your hands, as these actions may indicate that you are nervous and may even distract the interviewer. When talking to the interviewer, always look him or her right in the eyes.

As the discussion proceeds, conduct yourself just as you would in a telephone interview. Ask questions; get the interviewer to expand on the job so that you can answer questions accordingly. When feasible, answer questions by asking questions of your own:

"I see that you worked in the area of machine controls."

"Yes I have. Which kinds of control experience would be of most interest to you?"

In the event that there is a lull in the conversation, keep the discussion moving by asking questions: "Did you say that this job reports to the Office Manager?"

Answer only the questions that are asked and do not volunteer more information. If you sense that the interviewer is waiting for you to say more, ask another question: about the job, the level of responsibility, and the manner in which you would be evaluated. Should the job require you to relocate, you can also ask about the area, the cost of housing, and taxes.

Three things you must *not* do are: 1. to hog the entire conversation with your questions; 2. to give the interviewer the impression that you are trying to avoid giving information about yourself; and 3. to act like an interrogator.

Let the interviewer get a word or a question in at will. Do not answer every question with a question, but rather ask a couple of good questions at the beginning of the interview so you can get a definition of what the employer wants. This will give you the key to answering subsequent questions. After that, ask questions primarily to maintain control during the interview. As the interview proceeds and you are asked a question, answer it—directly and specifically. Just make sure that what you say is consistent with what employers want in general and consistent with what that interviewer wants in particular.

SMART ANSWERS TO TOUGH QUESTIONS

You're going to be hit with a barrage of questions during an interview. Some will be relatively easy to handle while others will be your downfall if you are not prepared. Earlier in this chapter it was shown that a difficult question can in some cases be handled by responding with one of your own. At other times, it may be more advantageous to give a straightforward answer.

"Why are you looking for a job?"

"I'm not. I'm just trying to find out if better opportunities exist elsewhere." If it's applicable to your career record, you can point out that you are obviously not a job-hopper.

If the employer presses you, you may want to go back to blunting.

"What makes you think things would be better here than where you are now?"

"Frankly, getting the answer to that question is my goal here today. How would you classify the opportunities here?" The answer you get should be fascinating.

You may also be asked how you got along with the people for whom you have worked.

"What did you like the least about any of the people you have worked for?"

"I don't know how to answer that question. I've liked each of my bosses."

How could an interview be complete without the question: "What would you like to be doing five years from now?"

You can respond "That's hard to say. I like the work I'm doing, but I also like being challenged and working with interesting people." That answer is fine if you do not have well-defined objectives or if your line of work is not one in which you are expected to move up the ladder. Secretaries, for example, are thought of by many employers as being life-long secretaries, with no potential for more responsibility. Such thinking is, of course, narrow-minded, but don't lose sight of your objectives: you are trying to get hired, not to change the world overnight. If you are in the kind of work in which people are not expected to grow, don't talk about your ambitious plans to take on greater responsibility.

A recent college graduate interviewing for a trainee's job, or even a junior executive with some experience can say "To be honest, I'd like to be in management within five years." Another way to answer career-objectives questions is to indicate that the job for which you are interviewing offers you an opportunity to progress into a certain kind of work that is more in line with your overall interests. Does the employer deal in a specialized service or product that would be a natural extension of what you've already done? A natural extension of skills you have already developed?

Have you been paying attention? The employer asked what you wanted to be doing five years from now, and you answered by saying that you wanted the job because of the business he is in. If that isn't conversational sidestepping, what is?

CONVERSATIONAL SIDESTEPPING

Asking questions and giving answers that don't address an employer's inquiries are both effective ways to sidestep an issue. When a direct answer would be embarrassing or even confusing, you sidestep by changing the subject or by putting the employer in the hot seat.

"I notice that you didn't fill in your date of birth on our application."

"I'm sorry. I didn't mean to be evasive. Is my age important?"

Or suppose an interviewer asks why you've had so many jobs in the past few years. What do you say? You won't look good if you bad-mouth any of your employers, and you certainly can't say that you couldn't get along with anyone or that you weren't able to do the work. How about this response?

"I *liked* working for my previous employers. I like working where I am now, but I want to do more. I'm certain I can handle additional responsibility but, realistically, there are no opportunities for growth unless I want to wait a number of years for someone to leave or retire. . . . I'm too young for that!"

Follow that with: "This job seems to have *good* growth potential!" Or, if more appropriate to what you already have been told, you can ask: "Can I *grow* with this job that we're talking about? I'm not looking for overnight promotions, but I *do* want opportunities."

See how it works? Sidestepping the question of your date of birth by asking whether it is important puts the employer in the position of being asked a question he does not want to answer. Turning a pointed question into a comment or question of your own about opportunities, on the other hand, forces the employer to sell himself to you.

Have you ever met interviewers who act as if they were trying out for a movie role as a tough district attorney? These guys are determined to give each job applicant an unmerciful grilling. You have to put the brakes on these characters so you get control of the interview before they do. Blunting their questions with your questions is one approach, but you can also effectively sidestep in several other ways. "Could you rephrase that question? I'm not quite sure what you mean." is one alternative; another is to change the subject by saying: "Before I answer that question, could I add something to what I said before?"

Chances are the person with whom you are talking will go along. Fine. Expand on an earlier point, talk about an additional strength you hadn't brought up yet, and tie it in to what you said before. You can also tell a short case history about something you've done; something that illustrates your capabilities.

Suppose an interviewer asks you to tell him something about your family. Seeming to be a perfect Mr. Nice Guy, this fellow wants to know how many children you have, their ages, and the age and occupation of your spouse. Isn't that nice? Maybe it is, but maybe this character is just snooping around for your age and whether you have personal responsibilities that might interfere with the job. If you'd rather not answer, tell a little story: "It's really eerie that you should ask those questions. I was interviewing for another job last week, and the office manager started to ask the same questions but the personnel director told him that he's not supposed to ask those questions before a person is hired. I didn't have any problem with giving the answers, but he took back the questions and we wound up talking about something else."

Short stories can be valuable, not only to sidestep questions and to show your capabilities, but also to illustrate your strengths in a way that shows the human side of your accomplishments. Just remember that there's a big difference between a short story and a novel. Stay brief and to the point: "This one customer wouldn't even talk with us. We were making no headway with this man until I remembered that price wasn't a factor with him; what he really wanted was color selection and quality. The first thing I did then was to find out whether our local distributor told him about our new rainbow process. It turned out that they didn't. Because of a mixup in their mail, they never got the notice of the new process. I caught the next flight out and the following evening, I was on my way home with the biggest order of the year."

SIDETRACKING

On occasion, you can sidetrack an aggressive interviewer by directing the conversation to an area that is of interest to both of you, but irrelevant to the interview. Typical possibilities are sports, movies, books, place you both have visited, office equipment, and any other noncontroversial subject.

When meeting on neutral grounds, look for clues in the interviewer's conversation. In his or her office, however, you should be able to spot a great number of clues. Look for awards, diplomas, photographs, desk ornaments, books, furniture, or anything else you could talk about. Maybe there are numerous pictures of the employer on a sailboat or on horseback, or maybe you see a society membership certificate like one you have. Seeing a diploma from a particular college, you could comment that you were recently on that campus, or you could ask whether the interviewer knows someone who you think went to that school at the same time.

Another way to sidetrack is to inquire about the history of the organization and to marvel about the company's accomplishments: "Have you always been at this location?" and "I bet it wasn't easy becoming the leader in the field" are especially good sidetrackers with top-management people who founded the company or have been with it for a long time.

The reason for sidetracking a persistent questioner is not to avoid his or her questions but rather to put at least part of the meeting on an even keel so that you are *not* on the defensive. If you can strike up a reasonable rapport discussing a subject of common interest, you will start to establish compatibility, and it is possible that the discussion may be more relaxed when you return to discussing the job. Should that happen, it will be because you and the interviewer will have become involved in a subject of common interest rather than merely in a job interview in which you each have different goals.

INVOLVE THE INTERVIEWER

You can talk *to* someone, or someone can talk *to* you, but the effects are the same; information flows in only one direction. What good is that? You should always try to talk *with* employers so that you each get the information needed to make the interview a joint success.

Such involvement is not only valuable with domineering interviewers, it's also a great help with employers who act as if they were made out of stone and their personality was like quick-drying concrete. You've met the type: expressionless, unemotional, and talking as if words were more precious than diamonds. These individuals are experts at one- or two-word answers and may be uncomfortable at interviewing. The only way to handle stonewall types is to get them involved by peppering them with questions and comments about themselves, their businesses, their accomplishments, and so forth. The more they open up, the more your chances are of getting clues as to what they want and the better your chances are of getting a foothold on compatibility.

PAY ATTENTION

Listening is a process that involves more than simply hearing what another person says, and watching is far more than looking at what someone else does.

Listening and watching are part of a process called *observing*. As it is used here, observing means interpreting and evaluating what other people say and do. We each have a tendency to hear what we want to hear, to see what we want to see, and to interpret events as we would like them to be interpreted. In other words, we jump to conclusions and we impulsively make erroneous decisions based upon what we would like to have happen rather than what is happening or what has happened.

This kind of impulsiveness leads to mistaken impressions of what an employer wants, incorrect assessments as to whether you are getting a favorable reaction, and eventually no job. You might as well go fishing! Impulsiveness can take over only when your emotions are in control. Don't let that happen. Put your intelligence in control, and you'll pay attention to what an employer says and does. You'll hear how your questions are answered, you'll see whether he is interested in what you are saying, and you'll know whether he fights or encourages an involved conversation; lastly, you'll know whether you feel comfortable with what you are told and compatible with the interviewer.

The first rule of paying attention is to look and talk as if you are paying attention. Eye contact is important in face to face meetings. You don't have to stare a person down with a menacing leer, but keep looking at the interviewer; it's a sign of assurance, interest, and nonevasiveness on your part. If you don't seem interested in the employer, how can you expect him to be interested in you?

As you listen, respond by occasionally nodding your head in an approving manner when the interviewer makes a point. Every once in awhile, you can also come out with a "mm-mmm" (emphasis on the "mmm"). To create the perception of indicating interest and agreement, you might even want to interject "Certainly," "Sure," or "Of course" when he finishes declarative statements. Beyond that, comments like "Oh?," "Really?" or "That's very interesting" not only show attention, but also encourage the other person to go on talking and giving you more information.

Also be aware of whether you have the full attention and interest of the interviewer. *After* you have made your pitch, it is easy to ruin a good impression by rambling on. Don't blow everything by failing to notice that you've gone through your whole story, and the interviewer is looking at his watch or is not as attentive as before. Repetition will not help, but you may save the day by shutting up, thanking the interviewer for his time, and gracefully leaving.

Before completing your sales pitch, you should follow a different set of rules. Someone who is looking around the room, checking the time, glancing at papers, and reading your application form is *not* paying attention to you. Make what you say more interesting; get the interviewer involved. Start talking about some topic about which you can establish mutual interest, based either on clues in his office, as we demonstrated in the discussion of sidetracking, or from his conversation. A sporting event, a recent news item, a new television program, or anything else that is noncontroversial is okay, as long as you can use it to get the conversation going in two directions with equal interest.

Pay attention also to the difference between facts and perceptions, and assume no more than you can from the information given. Don't let yourself jump to conclusions. If you are unclear about what an employer means by what he says, ask for clarification. If you aren't certain of what was meant by a question asked of you, request that it be rephrased. If you didn't hear something or can't see something, speak up. Even when you are certain of what was said, ask yourself: "What answer do they want?" If you aren't sure, ask for an explanation: "I'm not quite sure what you mean. Could you run that question by me again?" As long as you don't act like a nonstop dummy, it's perfectly okay to ask explanatory questions when necessary.

Watch for times when your message is not being understood or believed. If an interviewer's facial expression suggests doubt or disbelief, it is incumbent upon *you* to speak up if he does not seem to understand. "Is that clear?" and "You have some reservations about what I've just said, don't you?" are two ways of pulling potential negatives out into the open where you can deal with them.

Recognize and be receptive to what you have to do to establish personal compatibility with the interviewer. See the suggestions on page 49.

Table 1

Does the interviewer . . .	*If so, then you should . . .*
Tell jokes?	Laugh unless offended.

Table 1 *(Cont'd)*

Does the interviewer . . .	*If so, then you should . . .*
Brag how great the company is?	Be impressed and ask for more: "Really?" "No kidding!" "That's interesting. I didn't know."
Avoid eye contact? Talk in a monotone? Answer in one or two words?	Draw interviewer into conversation by involvement. Interviewer may be stonewall type. Don't ramble, don't repeat yourself, don't force him into corners with your questions, but ask enough so you can intelligently sell yourself.
Look at you with a piercing stare? Bark out questions? Seem annoyed at your questions? Ask direct, pointed questions?	Ask your questions and stand your ground, but do not challenge or confront. You cannot overwhelm a strong interviewer, but you *can* gain his respect. Blunt, sidestep, and sidetrack if you can.

Table 1 (Cont'd)

Does the interviewer . . .	If so, then you should . . .
Give vague answers? Sidestep or circumvent your questions?	Ask again. If you still get nonspecific answers, you're unlikely to ever get any explanations. Can you live with that?
Display no personality? Want to talk small talk?	Do exactly the same.

Make sure you don't gauge anyone by one statement or action. Look at several clues in context, and you'll be less likely to misread an interviewer's style and/or interests.

Do you know what to do if you're *not* meeting with the person making the final hiring decision? No? You haven't been paying attention. Go back and read Chapter 7.

MEETING CRITERIA HEAD-ON

An employer who firmly believes in the importance of "up-front" criteria may not let you sidestep your qualifications. Beyond that, maybe the thought of sidestepping and circumventing is not for you or you don't want to hide anything.

Either way, you can speak up for your accomplishments and concentrate on results. What results? Those that the employer wants achieved. Don't be arrogant or offensive, but show evidence and examples that give strong reasons why you can get the desired results despite your lack of some "up front" qualification. Your accomplishments, talents, and other strengths are not items you summarized merely for applications; they are also your heavy ammunition for interviews. Use that ammunition to illustrate that you are someone who *will* get the job done—not just in a passable manner, but on a basis that is outstanding, reliable, and thoroughly professional.

Still not making headway? Try a frontal attack: "I realize that I don't have a doctorate, but my experience covers every area you want handled and I'm an expert in each of them." If you still sense doubt, you could ask: "Could you give me an idea of which portions of the job you don't think I could do on a first-class basis without that degree?" Before you get an answer, you could add: "If you have any doubts about my capabilities, I'd be willing to document everything I've said."

SALARY TOPICS

For reasons that defy human intelligence, many employers can't get it into their heads that almost all employees work for their organization for one reason: they get paid for it. Telling an employer that a paycheck is your prime reason for work will accomplish nothing other than getting you a faster exit from the interview. Generally, employers do not want to hire people who are likely to ask for another raise every week. Some even object to raises on a yearly basis.

The best way to handle salary questions and salary negotiations is to deal from strength. An employer will pay you only in proportion to the potential value you offer the organization. The better the job you do of selling yourself and what you could do for the employer, the more you can get.

The hitch to all this is that the employer may ask about salary at the beginning, and if your figure is too high or too low, he may not be interested in talking further with you. This is particularly likely to be a problem in telephone interviews, which are used by many companies and agencies as a quick way of screening applicants who are not a good match. From their point of view, asking about salary is a way to ensure that they will not waste time talking to a job-seeker whose needs are not compatible with what the job has to offer.

When asked about salary over the telephone, you can try to defer the question by saying that your requirements are negotiable and depend on the job and its potential. Instead, you might turn the question of your salary needs around by saying: "I'm open to negotiation. What are you offering?" If you get an answer and it seems reasonable, you can then say: "That seems okay. That's about where I am now."

But you may *not* get an answer, and the person on the other end of the line may still be awaiting your response. Regardless of whether you were asked for your present salary or your salary requirements, you should answer as if you were asked to define your income needs. Then, give a range in approximate terms: "I'm looking for an income in the range of two fifty to three hundred a week." or "five fifty to six dollars an hour," "the mid-forties," "the low- to mid-twenties."

If you are still pressed, you can divulge your current salary as being in the lower end of that range. By predetermining what range to quote, you should be able to position yourself as looking for at most a modest income increase. As long as you quote figures that are plausible, you'll be on solid ground.

Would taking a job require you to relocate? You then have a good reason for not discussing salary. You can point out that a final determination of salary requirements would have to be based on your evaluation of differences in cost of living, taxes, commuting, and other factors. You can then suggest that the two of you talk further to see if it would be worth getting together to seriously evaluate each other.

As with all other aspects of the interview, you should not make more than one attempt to avoid an employer's questions; if he is hung up on determining your income, give an answer and make him happy.

In person, salary answers are easier to defer until later in the interview because whatever scheduling or traveling either of you had to do has been done and the interview is a *fait accompli*. The person you are meeting will not get up and leave if you attempt to put off the salary question until later. Again, saying that your requirements are a matter of the job and its potential is probably your best bet. When you do discuss salary, do it as described above, giving a range and claiming to be currently paid near its bottom.

Will that satisfy all potential employers? No. Some will want a more specific figure, so you'd better have something in mind before you go into the interview. Even worse, there are those employers who will ask for you to bring in your income tax forms for prior years as evidence of your current income and the growth of your earnings over the years. Horsefeathers! If the government wants to see your tax forms, fine. Ditto for your accountant. Prospective employers? Ask them why: why they need it and what it has to do with what you would do for them.

14. Wrapping It Up

The previous chapter was devoted almost entirely to the first goal of the interview process: selling yourself.

Without question, you will be forming opinions of both the job and the employer during the interview, but your second goal, that of determining your level of interest, should not be seriously pursued until *after* the first goal has been met. Should the employer volunteer information about vacation plans, medical insurance programs, and pensions, fine. Listen politely and attentively, ask questions if you need clarification, and act interested. It is also appropriate to ask about local housing, schools, taxes, and so on if you would have to relocate.

Until the employer starts to get serious, however, do not make an issue of any of these matters. Talking about living expenses and fringe benefits before you have an offer is like counting your chickens before the eggs are hatched. It also takes away from the time you have in which to sell yourself; interviews don't last forever, so why detract from your ability to meet your main goal? Lastly, you don't want to give the impression that you are hung up on anything but the job and the opportunities it offers.

If you want the job and the employer starts to negotiate with you or actually extends an offer, it's a different ball game. Now you know that you have sold yourself, and you have legitimate reasons for going into detail. How much you have to pay for medical insurance premiums has a direct impact on your spendable income, as do local taxes, commuting expenses, and parking costs if you drive. Similarly, there is no way you can evaluate a salary offer if you have to move for the job, and you don't know what the move would mean to you in terms of housing costs and general cost-of-living expenses.

Who pays relocation costs? In the case of most management or professional jobs, the employer usually pays, but not all employers have the same relocation policies. Aside from moving costs, there are real estate commissions to be paid if you have to sell a house, re-registration of auto license plates in different states, miscellaneous expenses such as for modification or replacement of carpeting or drapes that won't readily fit in a new location, new appliances that may be necessary, painting of the home you move into, and perhaps owning two homes at once if you have trouble selling your current home. Talk about the problems: can you get the down payment on a new home if you can't sell the one you're in now? What happens if you get in a bind? Will the employer bail you out, or will the seemingly positive act of accepting a job offer leave you with a pile of debts and other difficulties? Will the new employer pay for hotel and meal expenses you must incur while house-hunting? You'd better find out who pays for what before you take any action and before you accept the job.

Be particularly suspicious of any employer who won't give you straight answers and/or won't put the entire offer, including moving costs reimbursements, in writing. People can forget the details of conversations, and it is simply being prudent to get any offer on paper for future reference.

Presuming that you are satisfied with everything else, the most important aspect of sizing up a job is whether it involves the work you want to do and offers the opportunities you would like to have. Only you can answer that, but once you have an offer, do not hesitate to clarify any doubts you may have as to what you are expected to do, how much latitude you will have, responsibility or authority you would assume, and what guarantees you have or don't have for bonuses or raises. At this stage, you're not beating around the bush; ask the questions you need answered and as long as you keep yourself businesslike, you should get answers. Not getting answers should lead you to question whether this is the kind of person and company you would want to work for.

There is no way you can size up a job without also sizing up the person to whom you would report. Do you feel compatible with that individual? You don't have to like him, but do you feel you can get along and do you feel you can trust him? If you're convinced that you are not getting the straight scoop in an interview, what do you think you'll get if you take the job?

NEGOTIATING

Congratulations! You have an offer. Everything is in writing, you like the job, you like the employer, and the salary is fine; maybe even more than you hoped for. Great—take it!

But if the offer is poor or barely acceptable, you may be able to get more at this point than you could through raises a year or two from now. If the offer is at or very near the upper limit of the range you quoted, you can't turn it down gracefully unless you can come up with a reason. Possible examples are commuting costs, parking costs, or some other factor you can say you were not fully aware of earlier.

Should you find yourself in that situation of if you haven't been offered the upper limit of your quoted range, thank the employer and say that you are interested, but you'll have to do some thinking about the offer. Ask for a couple of days before giving your answer.

Be prepared at that point to be asked what you have to think about.

Ready as usual, you answer quickly: "I'm flattered with the offer and I like the opportunity you've laid out, but frankly, the money is a little on the low side. I'm just not sure it would be quite enough."

The employer might then attempt to convince you that it's a good offer or that he can't afford to pay more. Or, he might ask how much more would be "quite enough." If you quote a range, you just may get away with being offered the lower end of that range as long as the entire range is no more than about 10 percent of the offer.

Suppose, for instance, that you are offered an annual salary of $20,000. You have nothing to lose by saying: "I was really looking for twenty-one or twenty-two." If you're prepared to take the job anyway, all you can do is get more money or, if the employer isn't willing to budge, get the same as the original. Either way, you can still ask for time to make up your mind.

The employer may, of course, not respond to your request for time to think over the offer except by saying something to the effect that he'll look forward to your answer in two days.

It's decision time. Are you willing to take the job with the offer as it stands? Would you turn it down unless the ante is raised? Do you think you made a strong enough impression so that the employer would give a bit?

When the offer is nowhere near what you need to get by on, you have no choice but to make it clear that you cannot take the job unless the salary is raised. What good is the job if you have to starve to take it?

But suppose the offer is marginal. You'd rather not take the offer as it stands, but it's not really a bad offer and it may have good long-range potential What you may want to do is call back one day later, not two. Again you should thank the employer for the offer and *then* make your little speech: "It's an impressive opportunity, but I've got to live with realities. Unless my income were twenty-one or twenty-two thousand, I might be in trouble. If you can see your way clear to moving the offer into that range, I'll give you a definite yes right now!"

If the range isn't moved, you can remind him that you promised a final answer in two days and it's only one. Call back the next day, but no more hedging, no more give and take. Make your decision and stand by it.

One last comment on negotiating. if you've been out of work and need the money badly, take whatever you can get as long as you take it without having to move or get into any long-range commitment. Just because you take a job doesn't mean you have to stop looking for something better.

IF YOU'RE ASKED FOR A RÉSUMÉ

Some people simply cannot start a day without a cup of coffee. Similarly, some employers cannot evaluate a job candidate without a résumé. When asked for a résumé, say that you will be glad to put one in the mail as soon as you get home. If the interviewer's office is close to your home, say instead that you'll drop off a copy tomorrow morning.

As soon as you leave the interview, take notes of exactly what you said, and list those points that seemed to you to be of greatest interest to the interviewer. Then, when you get home, type up a short document custom-tailored to those points in a conventional résumé style. Add no new information not discussed in the interview and do *not* include any information that may have gone against you.

This after-the-fact résumé should be typed on your letterhead and should be completed on no more than one side of one sheet of paper. If you've done a good job of paying attention at the interview, you know what the employer wants and you can design your submittal accordingly.

Depending upon your situation, you may elect to choose either of two résumé formats:

- The chronological résumé, which lists your career experiences on a job-by-job basis. List only those jobs that substantiate similarities between what you have done and what the employer wants, indicating strong accomplishments in each case. This type of résumé is merely a re-listing of the "experience" section of a typical employment application form.

- The functional résumé, which lists accomplishments and employers separately.

An example of each of these résumés is given on pages 174–176. Since you submit résumés such as these after the interview, the choice of format is probably not critical, but the functional résumé may be more suitable if your career is varied or relatively short. This is because it lets you string out a number of achievements rather than a number of jobs, while focusing on your capabilities. The chronological résumé, on the other hand, probably does a better job of highlighting career growth.

Résumés sent in by mail or delivered to anyone other than the person who interviewed you should be accompanied by a very brief cover letter that expresses interest, thanks the interviewer for his or her consideration, references the enclosed résumé as promised, and offers to give additional information upon request. A sample letter is shown on page 177.

CHRONOLOGICAL RÉSUMÉ

Name   Address   Telephone

Education: Springdale, Ohio Public Schools
Graduated Springdale High School, 1966

Graduated Ohio State University
Bachelor of Science Degree in Behavioral
Studies, class of 1970

Professional Experience:

1970–1973 RMH Chemical Company, Dayton, Ohio. Regional
Salesman selling process by-products to
industrial and commercial research
laboratories in Ohio, Indiana, Kentucky, and
Michigan. Doubled sales in territory as a
result of identifying and capitalizing market
trends.

1973–1975 Armarc Group, Garnerville, New York. Eastern
Regional Sales Manager for manufacturer and
importer of pharmaceutical instruments and
analyzers. Set up a network of distributors
that increased total sales by 50 percent in
only eighteen months.

1975–1978 Joule Industries, Framingham, Massachusetts.
Sales Manager for environmental laboratories
manufacturer. Formulated and directed a
successful "target customer" program that
increased sales by 40 percent in one year by
penetration of 3,200 specific accounts
nationwide

Increased corporate sales by 64 percent in
three years while profits rose by 292
percent.

1978 to Present	EmBee International, Pikesville, Maryland. Sales and Marketing Manager for diversified design and engineering company engaged in energy exploration research. Simultaneously directed three separate national sales organizations consisting of 85 offices coast to coast. Increased primary market sales by 35 percent in seven months by proper analysis of trends in a previously declining market the company had considered abandoning.

Expanded company sales into new markets that now comprise 30 percent of national sales. Average total yearly growth of company sales is 19 percent since I took over sales and marketing management.

FUNCTIONAL RÉSUMÉ

Name   Address   Telephone

Personal Information:

  Born September 19, 1961, Bayonne, New Jersey
  Graduated Teaneck, New Jersey High School, 1978

Employed by:

  First National Securities Bank, New York City

Experience, Skills, and Capabilities:

  −Organizing and charting securities trading data.

  −Self-taught at operating IBM system 34 computer
   and programming with RPG II.

  −Liaison between traders, analysts, and backup
   support personnel to make sure that voice, data,
   and funds transfer communication lines are open
   and functioning at all times.

  −Training new office personnel in procedures and
   policies.

  −Currently assistant office manager in charge of
   communications.

  −Fluent in French and German.

  −Have written several articles for bank newsletter.

SAMPLE COVER LETTER

Date

Mr. Robert Etingill, President
Coalburning Wristwatches, Inc.
1107 Village Road South
Perth Amboy, New Jersey 04612

Dear Mr. Etingill:

Please accept my thanks for taking the time to meet with me yesterday. The opportunity to be Sales and Marketing Manager for your new line of watches is intriguing, and I have every confidence in my ability to meet, if not exceed, your expectations.

In accordance with your request, enclosed is a copy of my résumé. Should I be able to provide you with any additional information, please feel free to contact me again at your convenience.

Very truly yours,

FOLLOWING UP

Do yourself a big favor and, before you leave an interview, ask for a general idea as to when a decision might be expected. That way, you'll know what timetable to anticipate. One of the most frustrating parts of getting an employer to make up his or her mind is waiting for word on whether you are seriously being considered for the job. Back in Chapter 2, we referred to this frustration as the seventh step in the job-getting process.

You can follow up by contacting the employer after your interview, but letters and telephone calls are unlikely to have any effect on the final decision unless you have additional information to offer: information that you forgot about during the interview or that has come to your attention since then. Can you think of anything you didn't say that you should have said? How about something you did say that you probably should have clarified? Add and explain if you must, but don't ruin everything now. If you made a good impression during an interview, you might be best off leaving things as they are. If you made a poor impression, follow-up explanations probably won't help.

Watch for impulsiveness. Combined with your need to be safe, it might compel you to think that the employer lost your files and forgot your name. Pushing logic aside, you may then decide to write to the person you met, reminding him or her of the interview and launching into a long dissertation about how good you are. If you call and can't get through, you'll leave word but call back a dozen times before you realize that you are making a fool of yourself.

To follow up in writing, write just once and then send only an extremely short thank-you letter. Have you looked at the résumé cover letter on page 177? Remove the first sentence of the second paragraph and you have a two-paragraph letter that thanks the employer for meeting with you, expresses interest, and offers to provide any additional information.

If you *must* add new information, keep it short and to the point. Do not alibi shortcomings, do not plead; do not give the impression that you are changing the story you told in the interview, and do not show anything other than courtesy and confidence in your ability to do the job.

Prefer to call? Fine, particularly if you have another offer and must have an immediate decision or if the interviewer asked you to quickly get back to him with information you didn't have earlier. Just don't gab.

Has your call not been returned? Don't call back for a week. If you still can't get through, try once more a week after that and then forget it. After three calls in two weeks and no sign of interest, you can write that one off your list.

But you're not going to lose sleep over one employer, are you? You now know what you're doing, and there *will* be other opportunities.

Looking Up

You're a lot better off than you were before reading this book. You have saved yourself a great deal of time and trouble and—unlike most of the people against whom you will be competing—you now understand what job-getting is all about.

You know that getting a job has very little to do with competence in anything but knowing how to apply for jobs and how to control interviews. You also know that there is no reason why you should feel any less capable than anyone else in terms of your ability to get that job you want.

It is, of course, impossible to guarantee how well you can or will apply the concepts described on the foregoing pages. If you keep your intelligence in control and work diligently toward realistic goals, however, you *will* succeed.

Suggested References

FOR IDENTIFYING TARGET EMPLOYERS

Business Publication Rates and Data. Skokie, Ill.: Standard Rate & Data Service, Inc. Monthly.

Million Dollar Directory. Parsippany, N.J.: Dun's Marketing Services, Annual.

Standard & Poor's Register of Corporations, Directors, and Executives. New York: Standard & Poor's Corporation. Annual.

Directory of Directories. Detroit: Information Enterprises. Alternating years.

Adele Lewis, Bill Lewis, and Steven Radlauer. *How to Choose ... Change ... Advance Your Career.* Hauppauge, N.Y.: Barron's Educational Series, Inc., 1983

FOR LEARNING HOW TO WRITE BETTER

William Strunk, Jr., and E. B. White. *The Elements of Style.* New York: Macmillan, 1979.

Michael Montgomery and John Stratton. *The Writer's Hotline Handbook.* New York: New American Library, 1981.

Vincent F. Hopper, Cedric Gale, Ronald C. Foote, and Benjamin Griffith, *Essentials of English.* Hauppauge, N.Y.: Barron's Educational Series, Inc., 1982.

Robert M. Hochheiser. *Don't State It ... Communicate It!* Hauppauge, N.Y.: Barron's Educational Series, Inc., 1985.

FOR DEALING WITH EMPLOYERS AND OTHERS

Herb Cohen. *You Can Negotiate Anything.* New York: Lyle Stuart, 1980.

Tessa Albert Warschaw. *Winning by Negotiation.* New York: McGraw-Hill, 1980.

Robert M. Hochheiser. *How To Work For A Jerk.* New York: Random House, 1987.

Index

More selected BARRON'S titles:

DICTIONARY OF COMPUTER TERMS, 2nd EDITION
Douglas Downing and Michael Covington
Nearly 1,000 computer terms are clearly explained, and sample programs included. Paperback, $8.95, Canada $11.95/ISBN 4152-6, 288 pages

DICTIONARY OF FINANCE AND INVESTMENT TERMS
John Downes and Jordan Goodman
Defines and explains over 2500 Wall Street terms for professionals, business students, and average investors.
Paperback $9.95, Canada $13.95/ISBN 2522-9, 495 pages

DICTIONARY OF INSURANCE TERMS, by Harvey W. Rubin
Approximately 2500 insurance terms are defined as they relate to property, casualty, life, health, and other types of insurance.
Paperback, $8.95, Canada $11.95/ISBN 3772-3, 448 pages

DICTIONARY OF REAL ESTATE TERMS, 2nd EDITION
Jack P. Friedman, Jack C. Harris, and Bruce Lindeman
Defines over 1200 terms, with examples and illustrations. A key reference for everyone in real estate. Comprehensive and current.
Paperback $9.95, Canada $13.95/ISBN 3898-3, 224 pages

ACCOUNTING HANDBOOK
Joel G. Siegel and Jae K. Shim
Provides accounting rules, guidelines, formulas and techniques etc. to help students and business professionals work out accounting problems.
Hardcover: $24.95, Canada $33.95/ISBN 6176-4, 832 pages

REAL ESTATE HANDBOOK, 2nd EDITION
Jack P. Friedman and Jack C. Harris
A dictionary/reference for everyone in real estate. Defines over 1500 legal, financial, and architectural terms.
Cloth $21.95, Canada $29.95/ISBN 5758-9, 700 pages

HOW TO PREPARE FOR REAL ESTATE LICENSING EXAMINATIONS-SALESPERSON AND BROKER, 4th EDITION
Bruce Lindeman and Jack P. Friedman
Reviews current exam topics and features updated model exams and supplemental exams, all with explained answers.
Paperback, $10.95, Canada $14.95/ISBN 4355-3, 340 pages

BARRON'S FINANCE AND INVESTMENT HANDBOOK,
3rd EDITION. *John Downes and Jordan Goodman*
This hard-working handbook of essential information defines more than 3000 key terms, and explores 30 basic investment opportunities. The investment information is thoroughly up-to-date. Cloth $24.95, Canada $33.95/ISBN 6188-8, approx. 1152 pages

FINANCIAL TABLES FOR BETTER MONEY MANAGEMENT
Stephen S. Solomon, Dr. Clifford Marshall, and Martin Pepper
Pocket-sized handbooks of interest and investment rates tables used easily by average investors and mortgage holders. Paperback
Savings and Loans, $6.95, Canada $9.95/ISBN 2745-0, 272 pages
Real Estate Loans, $6.95, Canada $9.95/ISBN 2744-2, 336 pages
Mortgage Payments, $5.95, Canada $8.50/ISBN 2728-0, 304 pages
Stocks and Bonds, $5.50, Canada $7.95/ISBN 2727-2, 256 pages
Comprehensive Annuities, $5.50, Canada $7.95/ISBN 2726-4, 160 pages
Canadian Mortgage Payments, Canada $8.95/ISBN 3939-4, 336 pages
Adjustable Rate Mortgages, *Jack P. Friedman and Jack C . Harris*
$5.95, Canada $8.50/ISBN 3764-2, 288 pages

All prices are in U.S. and Canadian dollars and subject to change without notice. At your bookseller, or order direct adding 10% postage (minimum charge $1.50, Canada $2.00), N.Y. residents add sales tax.

Barron's Educational Series, Inc.
250 Wireless Boulevard, Hauppauge, NY 11788
Call toll-free: 1-800-645-3476, in NY 1-800-257-5729
In Canada: Georgetown Book Warehouse
34 Armstrong Ave., Georgetown, Ontario L7G 4R9